> Many children believe that life is long, while many older people believe that life is short. That's what I think.
>
> —Tsugumi Ohba

> There's no fantasy in this series, so I feel a bit nervous about it.
>
> —Takeshi Obata

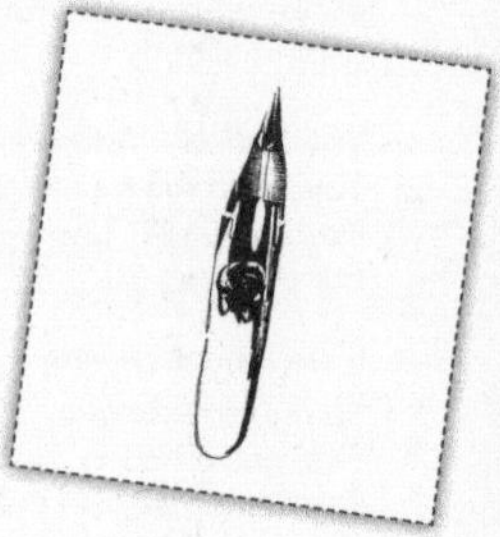

Tsugumi Ohba

Born in Tokyo, Tsugumi Ohba is the author of the hit series *Death Note*. His current series *Bakuman。* is serialized in *Weekly Shonen Jump*.

Takeshi Obata

Takeshi Obata was born in 1969 in Niigata, Japan, and is the artist of the wildly popular SHONEN JUMP title *Hikaru no Go*, which won the 2003 Tezuka Osamu Cultural Prize: Shinsei "New Hope" award and the 2000 Shogakukan Manga award. Obata is also the artist of *Arabian Majin Bokentan Lamp Lamp*, *Ayatsuri Sakon*, *Cyborg Jichan G.*, and the smash hit manga *Death Note*. His current series *Bakuman。* is serialized in *Weekly Shonen Jump*.

BAKUMAN。

Volume 1

SHONEN JUMP Manga Edition

Story by **TSUGUMI OHBA**
Art by **TAKESHI OBATA**

This volume contains material that was originally published in English in SHONEN JUMP #89–91. Artwork in the magazine may have been altered slightly from what is presented in this volume.

Translation & Adaptation | **Tetsuichiro Miyaki**
Touch-up Art & Lettering | **James Gaubatz**
Design | **Fawn Lau**
Editor | **Amy Yu**

Printed in the U.S.A.

Published by VIZ Media, LLC
P.O. Box 77010
San Francisco, CA 94107

10 9 8 7 6
First printing, August 2010
Sixth printing, April 2013

BAKUMAN。

1

DREAMS and REALITY

STORY BY
TSUGUMI OHBA

ART BY
TAKESHI OBATA

SHONEN JUMP MANGA

BAKUMAN。 Vol. 1

CONTENTS

DREAMS AND REALITY

SEVEN YEARS AGO
HA HA HA
MASHIRO
NOW HERE'S A GLASS FOR YOU, FATHER...
HA HA HA HA
CHAPTER 1
DREAMS AND REALITY
TAKA, I HEARD YOU GOT ANOTHER AWARD FOR YOUR ART.
OH, HI, UNCLE. YOU'RE HERE TOO?
I GOTTA SHOW MY FACE AROUND HERE DURING THE BON FESTIVAL AND NEW YEAR'S AT LEAST. HERE YOU GO...
New Year's Gift
THANKS.
WOW, LOOK AT THAT. IT'S GOT THE MINISTER OF EDUCATION'S NAME ON IT THIS TIME.
Testimonial
Third Prize
Moritaka Mashiro
Your work has been chosen for its excellence in the 11th Student Art Exhibition.

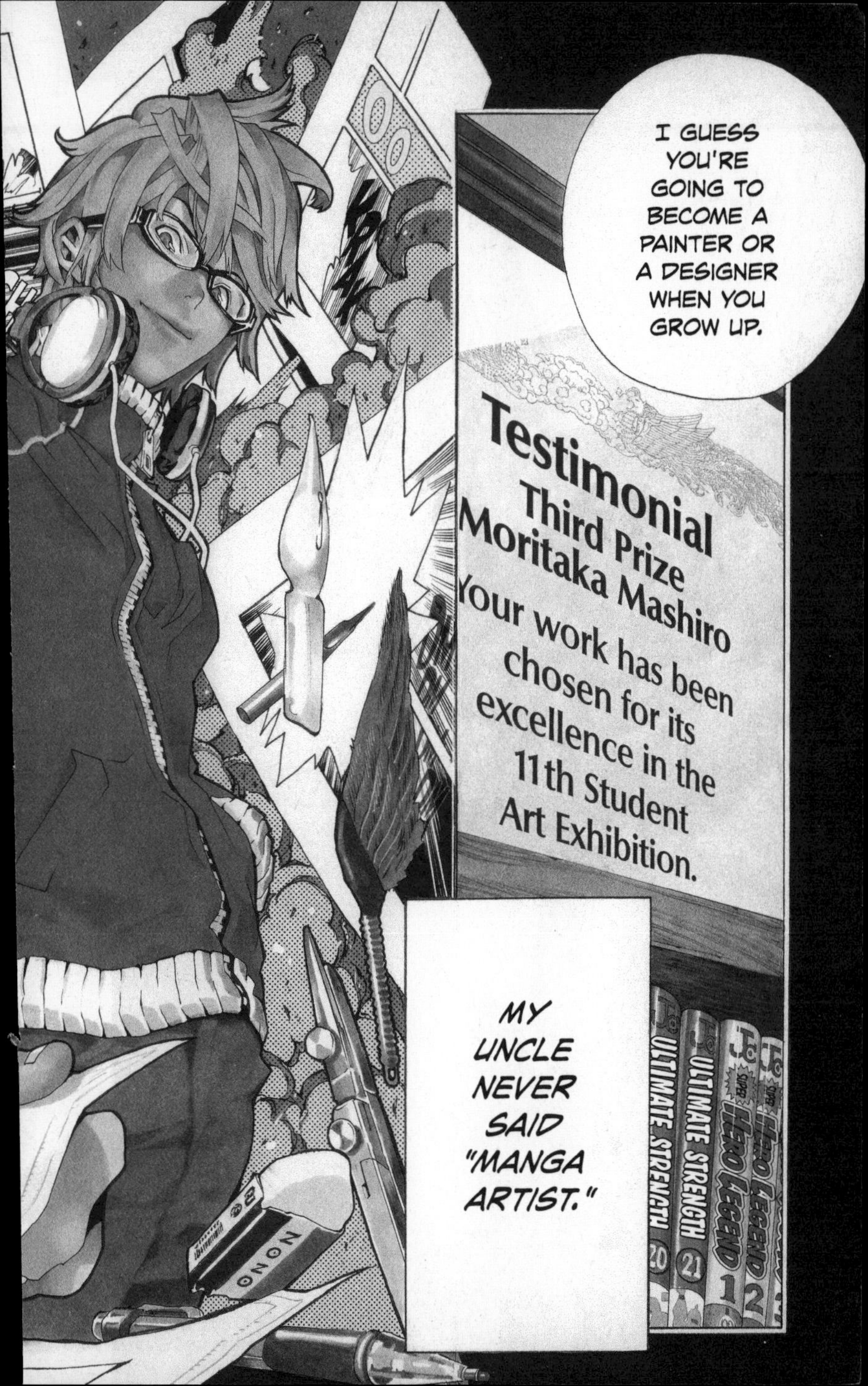
I GUESS YOU'RE GOING TO BECOME A PAINTER OR A DESIGNER WHEN YOU GROW UP.
Testimonial
Third Prize
Moritaka Mashiro
Your work has been chosen for its excellence in the 11th Student Art Exhibition.
MY UNCLE NEVER SAID "MANGA ARTIST."
ULTIMATE STRENGTH 20
ULTIMATE STRENGTH 21
SUPER HERO LEGEND 1
SUPER HERO LEGEND 2

THOK
VROOM
WHP
BOOM
INK
PENCIL
CHAPTER 1
DREAMS AND REALITY

BAKUMAN。

THOSE OF US IN THE LAST YEAR OF OUR COMPULSORY EDUCATION ALWAYS GET ADULTS ASKING US THINGS LIKE "WHAT KIND OF CAREER ARE YOU PURSUING?" OR "DO YOU HAVE ANY DREAMS FOR THE FUTURE?"
AND I, 14-YEAR-OLD MORITAKA MASHIRO, ALWAYS ANSWER WITH "I DON'T KNOW" OR "I HAVEN'T DECIDED YET."
THE **NORMAL** PATH MEANS GETTING INTO A GOOD HIGH SCHOOL, A GOOD COLLEGE AND A GOOD COMPANY TO WORK FOR.
SO I GUESS I'M JUST GOING TO LIVE A NORMAL LIFE.

I DON'T WANT TO CAUSE ANY PROBLEMS FOR MY PARENTS. I DON'T WANT TO BE CALLED A SHUT-IN.
THAT'S WHY I GO TO SCHOOL EVEN THOUGH IT'S SO MUCH EASIER TO STAY AT HOME AND SIT IN FRONT OF THE COMPUTER OR PLAY VIDEO GAMES.
I DON'T WANT TO BE CALLED A FREELOADER IN THE FUTURE, SO I'LL BECOME A WHITE-COLLAR WORKER EVEN THOUGH I DON'T WANT TO.
THE PEOPLE WHO MAKE IT TO THE TOP IN SOCIETY ARE THE GUYS WHO GET GOOD GRADES RIGHT NOW. WE'RE ALREADY SEPARATED INTO RANKS...
CORRECT. GOOD JOB, TAKAGI.
...SO IT'LL JUST BE AN EXTEN-SION OF WHERE WE ARE NOW.

READ THIS WAY

SHK
SHK
I RECENTLY READ IN A BOOK BY SOME PHILOSOPHER OR IDEALIST THAT SAID...
GLANCE
SHK
SHK
...THE GREATEST EVENT IN LIFE IS LOVE. IT LIFTS YOU UP AND PROVIDES MOTIVATION.
WHAT A JOKE. I BET THAT GUY HAD NO TROUBLE FLIRTING WITH GIRLS WHENEVER HE WANTED. FOR SOMEONE LIKE ME WHO DOESN'T EVEN HAVE THE GUTS TO SPEAK TO THE GIRL I HAVE A CRUSH ON...

READ THIS WAY

DONG
DONG
WORK HARD ON YOUR MIDTERM TOMORROW. YOUR GRADES AT THE END OF YOUR FIRST TERM WILL GREATLY INFLUENCE YOUR HIGH SCHOOL ENTRANCE RESULTS.
DONG
KLAT
KLAT
KLAT
I CAN'T BELIEVE WE'RE ALREADY THIRD-YEARS.
I DON'T WANT TO THINK ABOUT THE HIGH SCHOOL ENTRANCE EXAMS.
AAAAH, I JUST WANT TO PLAY VIDEO GAMES...

※"SAIKO" IS ANOTHER WAY TO PRONOUNCE THE KANJI CHARACTERS THAT SPELL OUT "MORITAKA."

SIGH...
THMP
TOMORROW, I'VE GOT JAPANESE AND MA...
HUH?
...
I FORGOT MY MATH NOTE-BOOK AT SCHOOL.
I DON'T NEED IT TO STUDY...
...BUT I DON'T WANNA LEAVE IT AT SCHOOL UNTIL TOMORROW MORNING.

READ THIS WAY

AKITO TAKAGI.
SHHK
WHAT ARE YOU DOING HERE? DON'T YOU NEED TO GO HOME AND STUDY TO KEEP BEING THE TOP STUDENT IN OUR GRADE?
SHUP
ACTUALLY, THE MIDTERM SHOULD BE EASY FOR HIM. HE'S JUST NATURALLY SMART...
SO WHAT'S HE DOING HERE ALONE ...?
!
MY NOTE-BOOK!

OH NO! THEN HE KNOWS I'VE GOT A CRUSH ON AZUKI...
COME ON, DON'T LOOK SO SERIOUS.
IT'S NOT LIKE IT'S A *DEATH NOTE*.
WHY DO YOU HAVE MY NOTEBOOK WITH YOU?
'CAUSE I SIT IN THE VERY BACK.
?
I KNEW YOU WERE WRITING SOMETHING IN IT WHEN YOU THOUGHT NO ONE WAS PAYING ATTENTION.
I ALSO KNEW YOU FORGOT IT AND WENT HOME.

SORRY, BUT I TOOK A LOOK AT IT AFTER EVERYBODY LEFT.
I WAS SURE THAT YOU'D COME BACK FOR IT THOUGH.
!
SO I'VE BEEN WAITING FOR YOU.
WAITING FOR ME? WHAT'S THIS GUY'S GAME?
YOU'RE REALLY GOOD AT DRAWING.
MIHO AZUKI, HUH? YOU'VE GOT GOOD TASTE. SHE'S RESERVED, SO SHE DOESN'T STAND OUT, BUT SHE'S THE CUTEST GIRL IN SCHOOL.
...
SO HE LIKES AZUKI AS WELL...

SHE PROBABLY HAS A CRUSH ON YOU TOO.
!
TH... THAT'S IMPOSSIBLE.
WE'VE NEVER TALKED TO EACH OTHER BEFORE...
AND HOW WOULD YOU KNOW SOMETHING LIKE THAT ANYWAY?
I TOLD YOU ALREADY.
I SIT IN THE VERY BACK.
SO YOU KNOW EVERYTHING ABOUT THIS CLASS BECAUSE YOU GET TO OBSERVE FROM THE BACK?
YEAH, PRETTY MUCH.
...

BUT IF YOU DON'T THINK SO, THEN MY WHOLE HUNCH ABOUT AZUKI HAVING A CRUSH ON YOU MIGHT JUST BE SPECULATION.
TCH. I WAS HAPPY FOR A MOMENT THERE TOO.
DON'T WORRY, I'M GIVING THE NOTEBOOK BACK TO YOU...
...AND I WON'T TELL ANYBODY ABOUT WHAT'S IN IT.
THANKS.
HOWEVER.
I DO HAVE ONE CONDITION.
HERE IT COMES.
WHAT?
THAT I GIVE AZUKI UP? I DON'T EVEN HAVE THE GUTS TO TELL HER MY FEELINGS ANYWAY.

I WANT YOU TO TEAM UP WITH ME TO CREATE MANGA.
I'VE ALWAYS LOVED MANGA, AND IT'S MY DREAM TO BECOME A MANGA WRITER.
I'VE GIVEN IT A LOT OF THOUGHT, AND I'VE DECIDED YOU'RE THE ONE. I NEED YOUR DRAWING SKILLS.
THIS GUY HAS TOP GRADES NATIONWIDE, AND HE WANTS TO BECOME A MANGA WRITER? IT'S HIS DREAM? HE HAS GOT TO BE KIDDING...

LOOK, GUYS HAVE TO ASPIRE TO BE RICH AND FAMOUS.
I DON'T HAVE THE LOOKS OR SINGING SKILLS TO ENTER SHOW BUSINESS, AND I DON'T EXCEL IN ANY SPORTS.
BUT I DO HAVE THE TALENT TO WRITE, AND YOU HAVE THE TALENT TO DRAW.
MANGA IS THE PRIDE OF OUR JAPANESE CULTURE! WE CAN BECOME FAMOUS THROUGH IT WORLD-WIDE!
MANGA
MANGA
SO YOU'RE GOING TO USE YOUR LAUDED WRITING SKILLS TO COME UP WITH THE STORY, AND I'M SUPPOSED TO DO THE DRAWING...
INTER-ESTING...
RIGHT?
"BUT I REFUSE."
"BUT I REFUSE"... SEE? I CAN TELL YOU'RE INTO MANGA.
SURE, TO *READ*.

IT'S IMPOSSIBLE TO MAKE IT AS A MANGA ARTIST. THE ONLY PEOPLE WHO TRULY DO ARE GENIUSES BORN WITH THAT KIND OF TALENT.
THE OTHERS ARE NOTHING MORE THAN *GAMBLERS*.
GAMBLERS?
A PROFESSIONAL MANGA ARTIST MAKES HIS LIVING PURELY THROUGH DRAWING MANGA HIS WHOLE LIFE.
PLEASE CHECK OUT THIS ARTIST'S NEXT SERIES!
Part 1 THE END
THANK YOU VERY MUCH FOR SUPPORTING THIS SERIES!
EVEN IF YOU SUCCEED IN PUBLISHING A SERIES FOR A WEEKLY MAGAZINE, YOUR MANGA IS RANKED ACCORDING TO THE READER QUESTIONNAIRES. IF IT ISN'T POPULAR ENOUGH, IT GETS CUT IN TEN WEEKS.
? HOW COME HE KNOWS SO MUCH ABOUT IT...?
YOU'RE A MANGA ARTIST IF YOU CREATE ONE MEGA HIT OR SEVERAL ONES SUCCESSFUL ENOUGH TO LIVE OFF OF. OTHERWISE, YOU'RE JUST A GAMBLER.
EVEN THE AUTHOR OF *DEATH NOTE* WROTE SOMEWHERE THAT HE'D PROBABLY STARVE TO DEATH IN FIVE YEARS IF HE DIDN'T KEEP WORKING.
HMM... THAT'S A SURPRISE. BUT THEN AGAIN, *DEATH NOTE* WAS A PRETTY SHORT SERIES.

PROBABLY ONLY 0.1 PERCENT OF THE POPULATION CAN TRULY BECOME SUCCESSFUL MANGA ARTISTS... ACTUALLY, 0.1 WOULD MEAN ONE IN A THOUSAND, SO IT'S MORE LIKE 0.001 PERCENT. ABOUT ONE IN A HUNDRED THOUSAND PEOPLE.
0.001%
Manga artists set for life.
IF YOU AND I TEAM UP, OUR INDIVIDUAL PROBABILITY'S DOWN TO 0.0005 PERCENT SINCE IT'S HALF THE REVENUE.
0.0005% Moritaka Mashiro
0.0005% Akito Takagi
YOU'RE CHATTY ALL OF A SUDDEN. AND WHAT'S WITH ALL THE STATS?
DID YOU GET THAT INFO FROM SOMEONE?
...
WELL, IT'S NOT LIKE HE'LL GO AROUND TELLING EVERYBODY...
MY UNCLE WAS A MANGA ARTIST... I MEAN, A GAMBLER.
THAT'S RIGHT. "WAS"...

YOU'RE KIDDING.
NOPE.
SHOOM
WHO?
I KNEW HE'D ASK...
YOU PROBABLY WOULDN'T KNOW. EVER HEARD OF "TARO KAWAGUCHI"? HE HAD A SERIES IN JUMP—
WHAAAAT?! I USED TO WATCH THE SUPERHERO LEGEND ANIME WHEN I WAS A KID!
I BOUGHT ALL THE COMICS AT A SECONDHAND BOOKSTORE WHEN I WAS IN SIXTH GRADE. I LOVE THAT MANGA!
HUH? HE KNOWS SUCH AN OLD SERIES? I KNEW HE WASN'T A TYPICAL NERD, BUT STILL...

THAT'S IT!
HUH? WHAT?
GRAB
YOU'VE GOT MANGA ARTIST BLOOD IN YOU, AND YOU KNOW A LOT ABOUT THE BUSINESS. PLUS IF THERE'S ANYTHING WE DON'T KNOW, WE CAN ALWAYS ASK YOUR UNCLE.
IT CAN'T GET ANY BETTER THAN THIS!
MANGA ARTIST BLOOD? HE'S JUST MY DAD'S YOUNGER BROTHER.
BESIDES, HE'S ALREADY—
I'M SURE IT RUNS IN THE FAMILY.
!
ACTUALLY, WASN'T TARO KAWAGUCHI KINDA BAD AT DRAWING? WHEREAS YOU'RE REALLY GOOD... MAYBE BLOOD DOESN'T HAVE ANYTHING TO DO WITH IT AFTER ALL...
SHING
IF HE THOUGHT HE COULD BECOME A SUCCESSFUL PRO WITH THOSE DRAWINGS, THEN HE WAS DEFINITELY GAMBLING.
...

I'D BETTER STOP TALKING ABOUT MY UNCLE.
AT ANY RATE, I'M NOT GOING TO DO IT. IF THAT'S YOUR CONDITION, THEN YOU CAN KEEP MY NOTEBOOK.
SEE YA, THIEF.
HEY, WAIT!
ARE YOU THINKING ABOUT PUTTING YOUR DRAWING SKILLS TO USE IN THE FUTURE?
NOT AT ALL.
THAT'S A TOTAL WASTE OF TALENT. YOU'VE STILL GOT SEVEN YEARS OF SCHOOL LEFT, SO IT'S WORTH A TRY, ISN'T IT?
SURE, IT MAY BE A GAMBLE. BUT IF YOU DON'T EVEN BUY THE LOTTERY TICKET, HOW CAN YOU EVER WIN?
IT'S THE SAME WITH MANGA. IF YOU DON'T EVEN DRAW THE MANGA, HOW WILL YOU KNOW IF IT'LL BE A HIT OR MISS? BETWEEN WINNING THE LOTTERY OR BECOMING A MANGA ARTIST, WHICH DO YOU THINK HAS A BETTER CHANCE?
BETTER CHANCE THAN WINNING THE LOTTERY...
THAT'S WHAT MY UNCLE USED TO SAY TOO...

GRP
COME ON, LET'S GIVE IT A TRY.
...
HEY, WRITING A BOOK REPORT AND CREATING A STORY FOR MANGA ARE TWO TOTALLY DIFFERENT THINGS...
I KNOW.
I WRITE MY BOOK REPORTS AFTER FIGURING OUT WHAT THE JUDGES WANT TO SEE.
SO ALL I HAVE TO DO NOW IS FIGURE OUT WHAT THE PUBLISHERS AND READERS WANT.
THEN WHY DON'T YOU JUST AIM FOR A LITERARY AWARD LIKE THE NAOKI PRIZE INSTEAD?
NAH. YOU MAKE MORE MONEY WITH MANGA NOWADAYS. PLUS I LIKE MANGA MORE.
IT'S LIKE A DREAM.
MAKE MORE MONEY... DREAM... SOUNDS JUST LIKE GAMBLING...

THEN YOU CAN DO THE DRAWING YOURSELF. OR YOU COULD JUST APPLY TO BECOME A MANGA WRITER.
THERE ARE MILLIONS OF PEOPLE WHO DRAW BETTER THAN ME, YOU KNOW.
WHAT? DO YOU WANT A STABLE JOB AS A CIVIL SERVANT OR SOMETHING?
I DON'T KNOW WHAT I WANT TO DO IN THE FUTURE YET... BUT YOU'RE SO SMART THAT I THOUGHT YOU'D WANT TO AIM FOR A JOB LIKE THAT YOURSELF...
THEN WHY ARE YOU SO AGAINST THE IDEA?
WHY...?
I'M NOT TOO SURE MYSELF...
...BUT IT'S PROBABLY BECAUSE IT'LL BE TOO MUCH OF A PAIN.
...
ZWAK...
I'M GOING HOME TO STUDY.
THANKS FOR THE NOTE-BOOK.

SO YOU'RE GOING TO END UP BECOMING A DULL BUSINESS-MAN?
THAT'S ALL YOU WANT OUT OF LIFE?
FOR A THIRD-YEAR STUDENT IN MIDDLE SCHOOL, YOU'RE UNIQUE FOR HAVING A DREAM YOU WANT TO STRIVE FOR.
BUT I'M NOT LIKE YOU. I'M NORMAL.
IT'S BETTER TO HAVE A HEAD START.
OTHER PEOPLE JUST KEEP DRIFTING AND GOING WITH THE FLOW SINCE THEY CAN'T DECIDE.

GIVE IT SOME SERIOUS THOUGHT. I MEAN, DO YOU WANT THINGS TO JUST STAY THIS WAY?
IF WE TEAM UP TOGETHER, I KNOW WE CAN DO IT.
YOU SURE ARE PERSISTENT.
OKAY, I'LL THINK ABOUT IT.
HUH, FOR REAL?
YEAH. BUT MY ANSWER IS STILL PROBABLY GOING TO BE NO.
THAT'S FINE. BUT I WANT YOU TO REALLY THINK ABOUT IT. IF YOUR ANSWER'S STILL NO, THEN I'LL GIVE UP.

MAS
UGH... I DON'T FEEL LIKE STUDYING...
KRASH
SLASH
SHNG
WSH
KLANG
MANGA ARTIST, HUH?
MANGA ARTIST ...

RREEEE
RREEEE
RREEEE
BACK IN ELEMENTARY SCHOOL, I WANTED TO BECOME A MANGA ARTIST.
RREEEE
THAT'S WHY MY UNCLE WAS MY HERO. I OFTEN DROPPED BY HIS STUDIO.
WHY DID YOU BECOME A MANGA ARTIST?
SKRCH
SKRCH
I'M ACTUALLY STILL A GAMBLER. NOT QUITE THE MANGA ARTIST YET.
OH YEAH. THEN WHY DID YOU BECOME A GAMBLER?
SKRCH...
'CAUSE I WANTED TO BE POPULAR WITH GIRLS.

MANGA ARTISTS ARE POPULAR WITH GIRLS?
Japanese Spirit
Wake up!
Just draw!!
1 page, 1 gag, 2 gags, 3 gags
STRICT DEADLINES!
I DON'T KNOW. I GUESS I MUST'VE THOUGHT I'D GET GIRLS IF I BECAME RICH AND FAMOUS.
KLAK...
DON'T TELL ANYBODY, OKAY?
Heh heh ...
WHOA, HE LOOKS WEIRD WITH THAT SMIRK ON HIS FACE...
THERE WAS THIS GIRL I HAD A CRUSH ON WHEN I WAS IN MIDDLE SCHOOL.
UH-HUH.
ZEBRA
WE BOTH GRADUATED WITHOUT EVER TALKING TO EACH OTHER REALLY.
THAT WAS A SHORT STORY.
FSH
BUT ON THE DAY OF GRADUATION, I GOT A LETTER FROM HER.
OH, A LOVE LETTER. THAT'S GOOD, ISN'T IT?

NOPE. IT ONLY SAID THINGS LIKE "LET'S BOTH DO OUR BEST IN THE FUTURE" AND WHATNOT.
HMM...
AND I WROTE A REPLY SAYING, "SURE, LET'S DO OUR BEST."
WE WENT TO DIFFERENT HIGH SCHOOLS, SO WE NEVER SAW EACH OTHER. BUT WE KEPT SENDING EACH OTHER LETTERS WITH THINGS LIKE "HOW ARE YOU DOING?" AND "GOOD LUCK." YOU KNOW, THAT SORT OF THING.
AW, THAT SOUNDS NICE. I GUESS IT WAS THAT KIND OF TIME.
YEAH... NO ONE THESE DAYS WOULD EVER DO SOMETHING LIKE THAT. TOO VEXING. ACTUALLY, NO ONE BACK THEN DID STUFF LIKE THAT EITHER.
ANYWAY, WHEN WE BOTH GRADUATED FROM HIGH SCHOOL, SHE ENTERED A TOP-NOTCH COMPANY, AND I GOT INTO A THIRD-RATE COLLEGE.

I SERIOUSLY WANTED TO MARRY HER BACK THEN. BUT I KNEW NO MATTER HOW HARD I WORKED, I'D PROBABLY JUST END UP AS A COG IN SOME SMALL, MEDIOCRE COMPANY.
I WANTED TO DO SOMETHING THAT WOULD GET HER TO NOTICE ME.
I DIDN'T HAVE ANY MONEY, BUT I FIGURED THAT AS LONG AS I HAD SOME PAPER AND A PEN, I COULD BECOME A NOVELIST OR A MANGA ARTIST. AND THAT'S HOW ALL THIS BEGAN.
WOW... YOU WANTED TO MARRY HER EVEN THOUGH YOU WERE JUST SENDING LETTERS TO EACH OTHER?
YEAH. WE NEVER WROTE "I LOVE YOU" ON THOSE LETTERS, BUT I'D BEEN IN LOVE WITH HER SINCE MIDDLE SCHOOL BECAUSE SHE WAS SO NICE AND REALLY PRETTY.
I THOUGHT I HAD A CHANCE 'CAUSE SHE KEPT WRITING LETTERS BACK TO ME.
WELL... I GUESS SO...

MONTHLY JUMP
MONTHLY JUMP
DURING MY FOURTH YEAR IN COLLEGE, I FINALLY GOT MY OWN SERIES PUBLISHED IN A MONTHLY MAGAZINE. I DECIDED TO CALL HER, THINKING I'D PROFESS MY LOVE TO HER.
COOL! SO?
I SHOULDN'T HAVE ASKED HER WHAT SHE WAS DOING.
?
SHE HAD BECOME THE COMPANY PRESIDENT'S PERSONAL SECRETARY. I WAS FLOORED.
THE THING IS...
...I WAS JUST A ROOKIE MANGA ARTIST DOING A MONTHLY MAGAZINE SERIES. I COULD GET AXED AT ANY TIME.
I THOUGHT THE GAP BETWEEN US HAD GOTTEN EVEN WIDER, SO I COULDN'T TELL HER MY FEELINGS IN THE END.
BUT *SUPERHERO LEGEND* BECAME AN ANIME, SO YOU TOLD HER AFTER THAT, DIDN'T YOU?
BY THE TIME THAT HAPPENED, I WAS 30 AND SHE HAD MARRIED SOMEONE ELSE.
OH NO...
SUPER HERO LEGEND

I GUESS YOU COULD SAY I LOST MY BET ON LOVE.
LOST...?
HOWEVER, I'VE BEEN ABLE TO COME THIS FAR BECAUSE SHE WAS AROUND. I CAN CONTINUE DRAWING MANGA WITHOUT GIVING UP BECAUSE I STILL BELIEVE THAT SHE'S WATCHING ME.
SHE CAN'T SEE MY PROGRESS IF I WAS JUST AN ORDINARY BUSINESSMAN, RIGHT?
HMM...
MY UNCLE TOLD ME ALL THAT WITH A SOMEWHAT HAPPY LOOK ON HIS FACE.
Wake up!
Just draw!!
EVEN THOUGH I WAS IN FOURTH GRADE, I COULD UNDERSTAND HOW HE FELT.

BUT TWO YEARS AFTER THAT CONVERSATION...
...MY UNCLE DIED. IT HAPPENED DURING MY LAST YEAR OF ELEMENTARY SCHOOL.
MY PARENTS TOLD ME HE DIED FROM OVERWORKING, BUT I THINK IT WAS SUICIDE. THAT'S A LOT MORE LIKE MY UNCLE SINCE HE ALWAYS SAID THAT LIFE WAS A GAMBLE. IT WAS ALL ABOUT WINNING OR LOSING.
You can no longer stand.
MORI-TAKA.
KNOCK
KNOCK
HUH? WHAT?
THE SERIES HE CREATED AFTER THE ANIME DIDN'T SELL AT ALL. AND EVEN THOUGH HE WORKED ON TWO MANGA SERIES IN SEVEN YEARS, BOTH OF THEM WERE SCRAPPED AFTER A SHORT WHILE. AFTER HE PASSED AWAY, WE FOUND OUT HE WAS DEEP IN DEBT TOO.
HERO LEGEND
Taro Kawaguchi
FOR ME, THE THOUGHT OF BECOMING A MANGA ARTIST DISAPPEARED THE MOMENT MY UNCLE DIED.

CHAK
HOW COULD YOU STAY OUT UNTIL EVENING WHEN YOU ASKED ME TO MAKE YOU RAMEN FOR LUNCH...?
!
WHAT ARE YOU *DOING*?! YOU HAVE AN EXAM TOMORROW, DON'T YOU?
YOU WON'T EVEN GET ACCEPTED INTO MINAMI HIGH SCHOOL AT THIS RATE!
SLAM
...
DOOT
GEEZ...
WHY CAN'T EVERY-BODY LEAVE ME AND MY FUTURE ALONE?

"I WANT YOU TO TEAM UP WITH ME TO CREATE MANGA."
"YOU WON'T EVEN GET ACCEPTED INTO MINAMI HIGH SCHOOL AT THIS RATE!"
"BUT I KNEW NO MATTER HOW HARD I WORKED, I'D PROBABLY JUST END UP AS A COG IN SOME SMALL, MEDIOCRE COMPANY."
"SO YOU'RE GOING TO END UP BECOMING A DULL BUSINESS-MAN?"
AGH!!
WHAM
...

VZZT VZZT ...
VZZT VZZT ...
I DON'T KNOW THIS NUMBER.
HI, IT'S ME. TAKAGI.
WHY DO YOU KNOW MY CELL PHONE NUMBER?
I ASKED SUZUKI.
THERE MUST BE A RULE AGAINST SOMETHING LIKE THAT...
ANYWAY ...
I'M GOING DOWN TO MIHO AZUKI'S HOUSE TO MAKE A CONFESSION TO HER, SO I WANT YOU TO COME WITH ME.
HUH?

HE KNOWS I HAVE A CRUSH ON HER... WHAT'S HE UP TO NOW?
W-WHAT, CAN'T YOU CONFESS YOUR FEELINGS TO HER ON YOUR OWN? THAT'S SAD...
THAT'S NOT IT. THIS IS GOING TO BE COMPLETELY MEANINGLESS UNLESS YOU'RE THERE TOO, SO I REALLY NEED YOU TO JOIN ME.
I DON'T GET WHAT YOU'RE TALKING ABOUT.
TRUST ME, YOU WON'T BE SORRY. AFTER ALL, I'M IN LOVE WITH YOUR DRAWINGS, AND I LIKE YOU.
ARE YOU OKAY? AREN'T YOU MAKING YOUR CONFESSION TO THE WRONG PERSON?
HUH? NO, THAT'S NOT WHAT I MEANT...
?
I DID A LITTLE RESEARCH ABOUT AZUKI AND FOUND OUT SOMETHING REALLY IMPORTANT. SO THIS CONFESSION IS A MUST!!
WHY DO I HAVE TO GO WATCH YOU CONFESS...?
JUST HURRY UP AND COME! I'LL BE WAITING AT ROWSON IN NISHI-CHO, SO MEET ME THERE, OKAY?
...
BEEP
DUU

WHAT'S HE SO EXCITED ABOUT? WHAT DID HE FIND OUT ABOUT AZUKI?
SHAA—
ROWSON
KLAK
ALL RIGHT! I'VE BEEN WAITING FOR YOU, SAIKO!
IT'S NOT SAIKO... IT'S MORI-TAKA.
AW, BUT EVERYBODY CALLS YOU THAT.
I DON'T WANT YOU TO...
C'MON, LET'S GO.
TMP
W-WHY DO I HAVE TO GO TOO?
IT'S JUST AROUND THE CORNER.
SWANKY PLACE. EXACTLY THE KIND OF HOUSE YOU WANT YOUR SWEETHEART TO BE LIVING IN.
I AGREE...

AZUKI
H... HERE GOES...
HAVE YOU EVER RANG THE DOORBELL OF A GIRL'S HOUSE BEFORE?
WELL, HAVE YOU? WHY DON'T YOU RING THE DOORBELL THEN?
AZUKI
NO WAY. YOU'RE THE ONE MAKING THE CONFESSION.
THEN JUST SHUT UP AND WATCH ME.
HERE.
PUSH
DING DONG
WHOA, HE REALLY DID IT!
I WANNA GO HOME!
GRAB
I WANT TO RUN TOO, BUT WE CAN'T JUST DITCH AFTER RINGING THE DOOR-BELL!

YES?
!
SHOOT, IT'S HER MOM!
U-UM, MY NAME'S AKITO TAKAGI, AND I'M IN THE SAME CLASS AS MIHO. THERE'S SOMETHING I'D LIKE TO ASK HER... ABOUT THE EXAM TOMMA...
... TOMOR-ROW...
HE STUT-TERED ...
TAKAGI?
AS IN THAT SMART BOY?
WOW, EVEN HER MOTHER KNOWS HE'S SMART. DOES THAT MEAN HER PARENTS WILL ALLOW THEM TO GO OUT...?
N... YES.
...
AZUKI
...?
HOLD ON...
OH, OKAY.
SHE'S SUSPICIOUS OF YOU, ISN'T SHE?
YES?
WHOA, THAT'S AZUKI'S VOICE...!

CAN YOU COME OUTSIDE? THERE'S SOME-THING IMPORTANT I NEED TO TALK TO YOU ABOUT.
TAKAGI HAS SOMETHING IMPORTANT TO TELL ME?
I DON'T LIKE THE SOUND OF THIS...
OKAY, I'LL BE OUT IN A MINUTE.
OHMYGOD! SHE'S COMING OUTSIDE! I WONDER WHAT KIND OF CLOTHES SHE USUALLY WEARS...
HEY, YOU SHOULD TELL HER THAT I'M HERE TOO!
SHOVE
OH.
YOU'RE RIGHT. SORRY, I'M KINDA PANICKING RIGHT NOW.
WELL, YEAH. THAT'S 'CAUSE YOU'RE GOING TO MAKE A CONFESSION TO HER...
CHAK
!

MASHIRO...
AZUKI...
HER TOP'S REALLY CUTE...
OH, NO... OUR EYES MET...
AND WE WERE STARING AT EACH OTHER FOR A FEW SECONDS TOO...
I-I'M NOT TURNING RED, AM I?

READ THIS WAY
SHUT...
GOSH... I HOPE I'M NOT TURNING RED.
...
I KNEW IT.
AZUKI...
YES?
I'M GOING TO BECOME A MANGA CREATOR. I CAME TO TELL YOU THAT TODAY.
?!
HUH?! WHY DOES HE HAVE TO TELL HER THAT?
UNLESS... THIS IS THE CONFES-SION HE WAS TALKING ABOUT?

I HEARD FROM YOUR FRIEND MIYOSHI...
...THAT YOU'RE TRYING TO BECOME A VOICE ACTRESS.
WHAT?!
A VOICE ACTRESS?!
UH-HUH.
"UH-HUH"?
SHE'S ADMITTING IT?
W... WHAT? SHE'S TRYING TO BECOME A VOICE ACTRESS? BUT... BUT HOW?
WHERE DID SHE EVEN GET SUCH AN IDEA? YOU GUYS ARE DREAMING TOO MUCH. WHAT ARE YOU, LOWBROW?!

YOU'RE REALLY SERIOUS ABOUT IT, SO YOU RECORDED YOUR VOICE AND TOOK IT TO VARIOUS PRODUCTION COMPANIES, RIGHT?
YOU HAVE GOT TO BE KIDDING ME. SHE DID THAT? I CAN'T BELIEVE SHE DID SOMETHING SO EMBARRASSING... I MEAN, THINK ABOUT IT— IT'S IMPOSSIBLE. YOU TWO HAVE TO BE MORE REALISTIC.
AND THE PRODUCTION PEOPLE THINK YOU'VE GOT TALENT.
HUH, SHE'S GOT TALENT?! THEN SHE'S REALLY GOING TO BECOME A VOICE ACTRESS?
OF COURSE I'D SUPPORT HER...
WAIT.
IF THAT HAPPENS, THERE'S GOING TO BE A HUGE GAP BETWEEN US. I'M JUST AN ORDINARY PERSON...
!
I THOUGHT THE GAP BETWEEN US HAD GOTTEN EVEN WIDER, SO I COULDN'T TELL HER MY FEELINGS IN THE END.

WELL... MASHIRO HERE HAS SOME-THING TO SAY TO YOU.
WHAT?
ME? WHAT DO I SAY?
THAT I LIKE HER?
I... I...
I'LL DO THE DRAWING, AND HE'LL WRITE THE STORIES.

OOH!
WOW! I KNEW IT! YOU GUYS ARE GOING TO DO SO WELL!
WHOA, HER EYES ARE SHINING. THEY'RE DAZZLING...
SO PRETTY...
S-SO WE WERE WONDERING IF YOU'D BE INTERESTED IN DOING THE VOICE OF THE HEROINE IF OUR MANGA EVER BECOMES ANIMATED...
TMP TMP
ARE YOU SERIOUS? I'M SO THRILLED YOU ASKED!
I'LL DO MY BEST!!

I PROMISE I'LL BECOME A VOICE ACTRESS SO I CAN BE IN YOUR ANIME. HOW WONDER-FUL!
SO IF THAT DREAM EVER COMES TRUE...

WHOOOA, SHE SEEMS SO HAPPY. SHE'S GOT THIS GREAT SMILE ON HER FACE. SHE'S LOOKING STRAIGHT AT ME, AND SHE'S RIGHT IN FRONT OF ME... SHE'S SO ADORABLE. YOU'RE REALLY CUTE... AZUKI...
THINGS ARE MOVING SO FAST, I DON'T KNOW WHAT'S GOING ON ANYMORE. THERE'S HER DREAM AND MY FEELINGS AND...
"THERE WAS THIS GIRL I HAD A CRUSH ON WHEN I WAS IN MIDDLE SCHOOL."
"I SERIOUSLY WANTED TO MARRY HER..."
"MARRY HER..."
"MARRY ..."
...WILL YOU MARRY ME?

HUH?
HUH?
HUH?
BLUSH
TMP TMP TMP
SHUT
WHAT IN THE WORLD GOT INTO YOU?
YEAH, WHAT THE HECK WAS I SAYING...? I'M JUST A THIRD-YEAR IN MIDDLE SCHOOL TOO...
IT'S BECAUSE OF WHAT MY UNCLE TOLD ME...
SHE MUST THINK I'M SUCH A MORON!
ARGH, THIS IS SO EMBARRASSING!
I HAVE TO TELL HER IT WAS A MISTAKE...

MASHIRO?
!
Y...! YES!
AZUKI
I'M SORRY. WHAT I SAID JUST NOW... I WAS...
OKAY. I PROMISE YOU.
HUH?
PROMISE? PROMISE WHAT?
...
Y... YOU DON'T MEAN MARRIAGE, DO YOU?
YES ...
WHAT!!
WHAT?!

SERIOUSLY, WHAT THE HECK IS GOING ON? WAIT, THIS IS A GOOD THING, RIGHT?
I GET TO MARRY AZUKI.
BUT ONLY AFTER OUR DREAMS ARE FULFILLED. I WON'T SEE YOU UNTIL THEN.
HUH?
AZUKI
WON'T SEE ME? WHAT'S THAT MEAN?
S-SO I WORK ON MY MANGA BECOMING AN ANIME, AND YOU WORK ON BECOMING A VOICE ACTRESS.
WE WON'T SEE EACH OTHER UNTIL THAT HAPPENS, AND THEN WE SUDDENLY GET MARRIED?
THAT'S RIGHT. WE KEEP STRIVING FOR OUR DREAMS WITHOUT LOSING FOCUS.
WHAT THE...? IS THIS SUPPOSED TO BE ROMANTIC?
IT'S A LITTLE EXTREME, ISN'T IT?

UNTIL THEN, WE CAN ENCOURAGE EACH OTHER THROUGH EMAIL.
IT'S NICE THAT WE CAN ENCOURAGE EACH OTHER...
BUT WHY IS IT THROUGH EMAIL AND NOT PHONE CALLS?
MAYBE SHE REALIZED THAT WE'D BOTH BE TOO EMBARRASSED TO TALK ON THE PHONE?
I HARDLY GOT TO TALK TO HER UNTIL NOW, SO JUST BEING ABLE TO SEND MESSAGES TO HER IS...
OH! THIS IS...
...JUST LIKE MY UNCLE...
?
SO THIS IS WHAT HE MEANT.
I GET IT. I GET IT NOW, UNCLE.
YOU HAD AN INNOCENT, WONDERFUL RELATIONSHIP LIKE THIS TOO, DIDN'T YOU?
BUT I ACTUALLY GOT HER TO PROMISE TO MARRY ME ONCE OUR DREAMS COME TRUE.
I THINK I'VE GOT BETTER ODDS THAN YOU DID.

IS THAT OKAY?
YES, THAT'S FINE WITH ME. I'M BETTING ON IT! I MEAN, LET'S GO FOR IT!
OH, MY MOTHER'S COMING. BYE.
BEEP
I'M GOING TO BECOME A MANGA ARTIST.
YEAH.
THINGS TURNED OUT LIKE I THOUGHT THEY WOULD. ACTUALLY, BETTER THAN I EXPECTED, SAIKO.
WE'RE GOING TO BECOME THE BEST MANGA CREATORS IN JAPAN EVER!
THAT'S IMPOSSIBLE. THE BIRTH RATE IN THIS COUNTRY IS DECLINING, SO IT ISN'T FEASIBLE TO BEAT *DRAGON BALL* OR *ONE PIECE* NOW.
SHOOM
YOU'RE SO ANALYTICAL.
BESIDES, I SAID I WAS GOING TO BECOME A MANGA ARTIST. I NEVER PROMISED I WAS GOING TO TEAM UP WITH ***YOU***.
WHAAAAAT?!
I'M GOING TO DROP BY THE BOOKSTORE AND GO HOME.
HEY, SAIKO...

COME TO THINK OF IT, I DON'T KNOW MIHO'S CELL PHONE NUMBER OR HER EMAIL ADDRESS.
AND WE'RE STILL GOING TO SEE EACH OTHER AT SCHOOL TOO...
MAYBE SHE MEANT WE WOULDN'T SEE EACH OTHER ALONE IN PRIVATE?
WELL, THAT'S NOT IMPORTANT FOR NOW.
I'M GOING TO BECOME A MANGA ARTIST!
AND I'M GOING TO MARRY AZUKI!!
本 BOOKS
MANGA NO OUJA
KING OF MANGA
Vol. 1
Beginner's Book
MAYO & MR. RABBIT'S HOW-TO-DRAW-MANGA SCHOOL
Let's become manga artists!!
SHOOOM

OHBA'S STORYBOARD

BAKUMAN。vol.1

"Until the Final Draft Is Complete"

Chapter 1, pp. 56-57 and pp. 58-59

※CREATOR STORYBOARDS AND FINISHED PAGES IN JAPANESE

OBATA'S STORYBOARD

COMPLETE!

OBATA'S STORYBOARD

COMPLETE!

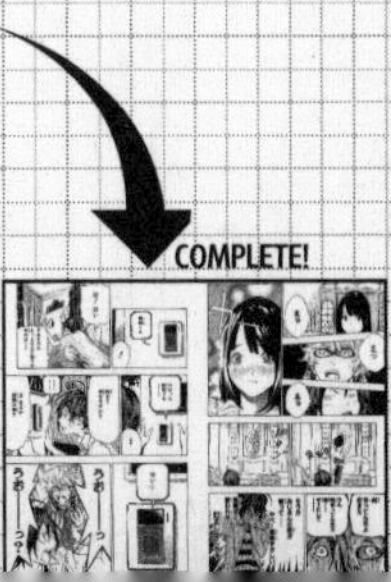

CHAPTER 2
DUMB AND SMART

MASHIR
MORITAKA... TAKAGI IS WAITING FOR YOU DOWNSTAIRS, SO HURRY UP AND GET READY.
HUH?
SHA
HE'S SO ANNOYING ...

※"SAIKO" MEANS "EXCELLENT" IN JAPANESE.

SAIKO, YOUR UNCLE DIED THREE YEARS AGO, RIGHT?
YOU LOOKED IT UP?
WE LIVE IN THE NEIGHBORHOOD, SO MY PARENTS KNEW WHEN YOUR UNCLE DIED. THEY DIDN'T KNOW HE WAS THE MANGA ARTIST TARO KAWAGUCHI THOUGH.
JUMP COMICS
HERO LEGEND
Kawaguchi
THAT'S BECAUSE TARO KAWAGUCHI IS HIS PEN NAME. HIS REAL NAME IS NOBUHIRO MASHIRO. THERE WAS A SMALL ARTICLE IN THE CORNER OF SOME NEWSPAPER ENTITLED "DEATH OF A MANGA ARTIST"...
A MANGA ARTIST WHO DOESN'T WORK IS THE SAME AS BEING A LEECH.
AND WHEN THAT SITUATION CONTINUES FOR SEVEN YEARS, IT'S NO SURPRISE THAT HE'D WANT TO HANG HIMSELF.
HE COMMITTED SUICIDE?
MY PARENTS SAID HE DIED OF OVERWORK, BUT HOW COULD THAT BE WHEN HE DIDN'T HAVE A JOB FOR SEVEN YEARS?

WELL, EVEN IF YOU DON'T PLAN ON GOING THROUGH WITH IT, I'M STILL GOING TO DO IT.
IT MIGHT BE INTERESTING TO SEE YOU HANG YOURSELF... BUT MAYBE YOU DON'T WANT TO BE A MANGA ARTIST NOW, SHUJIN?
I HAVEN'T SAID THAT I'LL COLLABORATE WITH YOU YET.
NO WAY! OF COURSE I'LL DO IT. I'M GONNA TEAM UP WITH YOU SO WE CAN BECOME THE GREATEST MANGA ARTISTS IN JAPAN!
WHAT, THIS AGAIN? I'M THE ONE WHO GOT YOU ALL FIRED UP, AREN'T I?
I DO HAVE MUCH GRATITUDE FOR YOU PLAYING CUPID THOUGH, SHUJIN.
...
IT WASN'T YOU. IT WAS AZUKI.
WHAAT?!

AZUKI...
DONG
DONG
DONG
DONG
OKAY, YOU CAN START.
SHE'S ACTING THE SAME AS ALWAYS...
EVEN AFTER EVERYTHING THAT HAPPENED YESTERDAY...

BLUSH
"SO IF THAT DREAM EVER COMES TRUE, WILL YOU MARRY ME?"
"OKAY. I PROMISE YOU."
"WE KEEP STRIVING FOR OUR DREAMS WITHOUT LOSING FOCUS."
SHE'LL BECOME A VOICE ACTRESS... I'LL BECOME A MANGA ARTIST...
DREAMS... MARRIAGE...
I GET TO MARRY AZUKI...
B-BMP B-BMP B-BMP B-BMP B-BMP
UGH...
THIS IS NO GOOD...

SIR.
WOBBLE...
WHAT IS IT, MASHIRO?
I DON'T FEEL WELL, SO MAY I REST IN THE NURSE'S OFFICE UNTIL THE NEXT CLASS?
...
HE PROBABLY COULDN'T SLEEP LAST NIGHT.
YOUR FACE DOES LOOK A LITTLE PALE. I CAN LET YOU TAKE A MAKEUP EXAM LATER IF YOU WANT TO.
THAT'S OKAY. I FINISHED HALF THE TEST, SO THIS'LL BE FINE.
KLAK
SHHK..
I WONDER WHAT'S WRONG WITH MASHIRO?
I HOPE HE'S OKAY...

READ THIS WAY
EXCUSE ME, SIR... I PULLED AN ALL-NIGHTER AND FEEL A LITTLE DIZZY NOW, SO CAN I GO TOO?
ACTUALLY I SLEPT A LOT LAST NIGHT.
I FINISHED THE TEST.
YOU TOO, TAKAGI? WELL, GO AHEAD, I GUESS...
MASHIRO AND TAKAGI...
...
"SIR, I WANT TO GO TOO." JUST KIDDING...
TEE HEE
NURSE'S OFFICE
WHAT? YOU TOO, TAKAGI?
SORRY, I DIDN'T GET MUCH SLEEP LAST NIGHT, SO I'M GOING TO BORROW THE BED.
!
TAKAGI?

SHUP
YOU OKAY, SAIKO?
HE REALLY DOES LIKE TO POKE HIS NOSE INTO THINGS.
I CAN'T BREATHE INSIDE THAT CLASSROOM.
CAN'T BREATHE? BECAUSE YOU DIDN'T SLEEP WELL LAST NIGHT?
...
IT FEELS LIKE SOMETHING'S GRIPPING MY CHEST WHEN I'M IN THE SAME ROOM AS AZUKI...
AH HA HA HA!

NO PLAYING AROUND!!
S- SORRY.
SOMETHING GRIPPING YOUR CHEST, HUH? I GUESS THAT MEANS YOU GUYS MADE SOME PROGRESS IN YOUR RELATIONSHIP.
WHAT DO YOU MEAN? NOTHING'S CHANGED.
NOTHING'S CHANGED? THEN WHAT DID YOU GUYS TALK ABOUT AFTER EXCHANGING EMAIL ADDRESSES?
WE HAVEN'T EXCHANGED ANYTHING.
WHAT?!
HEY, IF YOU'VE GOT ENOUGH STAMINA TO CHAT, THEN GO BACK TO YOUR CLASS-ROOM!
WE CAN'T TALK IN HERE. LET'S GO OUTSIDE.
OKAY.
THANK YOU VERY MUCH. WE'RE HEADING BACK NOW.
SHHK...
WHAT DID YOU GUYS COME HERE FOR? YOU WERE ONLY HERE FOR LIKE THREE MINUTES ...

I'LL GET AZUKI'S EMAIL ADDRESS FOR YOU.
DON'T WORRY ABOUT IT. SHE'LL THINK I'M HOPELESS IF I HAD YOU DO THAT.
BUT YOU CAN'T ASK HER YOURSELF, CAN YOU?
IF I COULD TALK TO HER THAT EASILY, I WOULDN'T BE IN THIS PREDICAMENT.
...
SAIKO...
YOU REALLY LIKE HER, DON'T YOU.

Y-YEAH.
WHY DO YOU THINK I ASKED HER TO MARRY ME?
I REALLY LIKE PEOPLE LIKE YOU AND AZUKI.
PEOPLE LIKE ME AND AZUKI?
WHAT DO YOU MEAN, YOU LIKE US? YOU REALLY ARE A WEIRD GUY, YOU KNOW.
WELL, LOOK AT ALL THE OTHER THIRD-YEAR GUYS WHO ARE DATING GIRLS. THEY'RE ALL LIKE, "WE'VE GONE ALL THE WAY."
MOST OF THEM PRETTY MUCH BRAG ABOUT IT.
I MUCH PREFER A GUY WHO FEELS LOVESICK SIMPLY BECAUSE THE GIRL HE HAS A CRUSH ON IS IN THE SAME ROOM AS HIM.
WELL, WHAT ABOUT IT? IT'S NOT LIKE I FEEL HAPPY THAT YOU LIKE ME.
BUT THIS MEANS THAT YOU AND I ARE GOING TO TEAM UP.
HOW DO YOU FIGURE?
I'M THE ONLY PERSON WHO KNOWS YOU'RE IN LOVE WITH AZUKI, RIGHT?
YEAH. DON'T TELL ANYBODY.

THAT MEANS I'M THE ONLY GUY YOU CAN TELL YOUR PROBLEMS TO ABOUT YOUR RELATIONSHIP.
I'LL BE YOUR VERY BEST FRIEND.
WE CAN WORK ON YOUR ROMANCE AND THE MANGA TOGETHER!
LOVE IS LOVE, AND MANGA IS MANGA.
TUP
IS THAT SO?
HEY, DON'T YOU NEED TO GO BACK TO THE CLASSROOM?
I ACED THE TEST. PERFECT SCORE, I'M SURE OF IT.
I DON'T GET IT. WHY DO YOU HAVE TO STUDY SO HARD IF YOU WANT TO BECOME A MANGA ARTIST?
YOU DON'T NEED TO HAVE A HIGH EDUCATIONAL BACKGROUND, YOU KNOW.
INSURANCE.
I'M NOT 100 PERCENT SURE THAT I'LL BECOME A MANGA ARTIST EITHER.

I THOUGHT SO... THAT'S THE SMART WAY TO LIVE.
DO ALL THE OTHER GUYS IN CLASS LOOK DUMB TO YOU?
HUH?
DO YOU THINK YOU'RE THE SMARTEST GUY IN CLASS?
WHAT'S WITH THIS ALL OF A SUDDEN? THAT ISN'T A VERY NICE QUESTION.
IS THAT A YES?
DO YOU THINK YOU NEED TO BE SMART TO BECOME A MANGA ARTIST?
!
I DO. AT LEAST, YOU CAN'T BECOME ONE IF YOU'RE DUMB.
ALL RIGHT. IF THAT'S WHAT YOU MEANT BY THAT QUESTION, THEN I'LL ANSWER IT.
I DON'T THINK GETTING GOOD GRADES MEANS YOU'RE SMART...
...BUT I DO THINK THAT I'M THE THIRD SMARTEST KID IN OUR CLASS.
THIRD? THAT'S VERY MODEST OF YOU.
WHO ARE THE TWO PEOPLE SMARTER THAN YOU?

YOU AND AZUKI.
WHAT?
OKAY, YOU ARE DUMB...
YOU'RE SMART, SAIKO. I'VE ONLY BEEN IN THAT CLASS WITH YOU FOR LESS THAN TWO MONTHS, BUT IT WAS OBVIOUS TO ME FROM THE START.
I DIDN'T DRAG YOU INTO THIS JUST BECAUSE YOU'RE GOOD AT DRAWING. I WANTED SOMEONE WITH BRAINS AND GOOD TASTE, SO THAT'S WHY I CHOSE YOU.
BESIDES, YOU CAN'T ASK THAT QUESTION ABOUT THE GUYS IN OUR CLASS BEING DUMB...
... UNLESS THAT'S WHAT YOU PERSONALLY THINK, SAIKO.
HE REALLY IS SMART.
...
OKAY, FORGET ME FOR A MOMENT.
AZUKI ISN'T THAT SMART, IS SHE? SHE SEEMS TO STUDY A LOT, BUT HER GRADES ARE JUST ABOVE AVERAGE.
PLUS SHE WANTS TO BECOME A VOICE ACTRESS... THAT'S RATHER DUMB, ISN'T IT?
SHE'S PROBABLY JUST PRETENDING TO STUDY.

PRETENDING?
THE REAL DUMB STUDENTS ARE THOSE WHO TAKE PERFECT NOTES IN CLASS, ASK THE TEACHER QUESTIONS, STUDY AT HOME, BUT STILL GET LOW GRADES.
WELL, YEAH...
AZUKI ISN'T CALCULATING. SHE'S JUST BEING A GIRL IN A NATURAL WAY.
HUH? I DON'T GET IT. EXPLAIN.
HOW DO I PUT IT? AZUKI NATURALLY KNOWS THAT A GIRL SHOULD BE GRACEFUL AND POLITE...
...AND BECAUSE SHE IS A GIRL, SHE SHOULD BE EARNEST ABOUT THINGS AND GET AVERAGE GRADES. SHE KNOWS BY INSTINCT THAT A GIRL WON'T LOOK CUTE IF SHE'S OVERLY SMART.
THAT IN AND OF ITSELF MEANS SHE'S SMART, RIGHT?
HMM. AREN'T YOU READING TOO MUCH INTO IT?
NO, I'M NOT. AZUKI'S ATTRACTIVE BECAUSE SHE'S SMART.

YOU SAW HER HOUSE, DIDN'T YOU? I DON'T KNOW WHAT HER PARENTS DO, BUT YOU CAN'T HAVE A HOUSE THAT LARGE UNLESS YOU EXCEL AT SOMETHING. THAT, OR YOU'RE DOING SOMETHING ILLEGAL.
AND EVEN IF IT IS SOMETHING ILLEGAL, THEY HAVEN'T BEEN CAUGHT, SO THAT'S PRETTY AMAZING TOO.
IT'S ALL IN THE BLOOD.
THERE YOU GO AGAIN, TALKING ABOUT BLOODLINES. SO SHE'S SMART BECAUSE HER DAD'S SMART...? IT'S A SIMPLE IDEA, BUT I GUESS YOUR PARENTS ARE IMPORTANT...
I LIKE 10,000 YEN BILLS, BUT I DON'T LIKE YUKICHI FUKUZAWA.*
HE WROTE, "HEAVEN DOES NOT CREATE ONE MAN ABOVE OR BELOW ANOTHER MAN," BUT I REALLY THINK HE SHOULD HAVE ADDED, "IF ONLY THAT WERE TRUE" AFTER THAT SENTENCE.
HAHA, I GET IT. IT'S NOT HEAVEN THAT CREATES YOU BUT YOUR PARENTS. AND THE STATUS OF YOUR PARENTS WILL CREATE A DIFFERENCE BETWEEN YOU AND OTHERS FROM THE MOMENT YOU'RE BORN.
*YUKICHI FUKUZAWA'S IMAGE IS ON THE 10,000 YEN BILL.

READ THIS WAY
THE REASON SHE'S THINKING ABOUT BECOMING A VOICE ACTRESS IS SHE NATURALLY CHOSE A DREAM THAT MANY GIRLS HAVE NOWADAYS, AND SHE'S JUST TRYING TO FULLY ENJOY HER LIFE AS A GIRL.
SHE DOESN'T FEEL ANY PRESSURE LIKE WE DO ABOUT OUR FUTURE AND WHATNOT.
BECAUSE SHE'S A GIRL?
THAT'S RIGHT. SHE KNOWS WHAT IT MEANS TO BE A GIRL. SHE KNOWS BY INSTINCT THAT THE BEST THING FOR A GIRL IS TO GET MARRIED AND BECOME SOMEBODY'S WIFE...
...AND UNTIL THEN— NO, EVEN AFTER SHE'S MARRIED, SHE'LL REMAIN GRACEFUL AND POLITE.
AND SHE DOES ALL THAT WITHOUT CALCULATION, SO SHE'S A HUNDRED TIMES SMARTER THAN IWASE, THE GIRL WITH THE BEST GRADES IN CLASS.
NO MATTER HOW CUTE A GIRL IS, YOU CAN'T REALLY LIKE HER IF SHE'S UTTERLY DUMB, RIGHT?
THE SAME GOES FOR THE OPPOSITE. IWASE IS PRETTY GOOD-LOOKING, BUT SHE'S NOT VERY LIKABLE, IS SHE?
SHE'S THE SMARTEST GIRL IN CLASS GRADE-WISE, BUT I DON'T LIKE HOW SHE TAKES PRIDE IN THAT. THAT'S WHY I ACTUALLY THINK SHE'S DUMB.

I SAID AZUKI'S ATTRACTIVE TOO, DIDN'T I? SHE'S ATTRACTIVE BECAUSE SHE HAS CLASS. THAT COMES FROM HER FAMILY AND BECAUSE SHE'S UNDERSTANDING AND SMART.
CLASS, HUH?
YOU SURE DO HAVE HIGH PRAISE FOR HER.
AND EVEN THOUGH I PRAISE HER, YOU DON'T GET JEALOUS BECAUSE YOU'RE SMART.
AKITO TAKAGI IS SO MUCH SMARTER THAN ME.
AND THE WAY HE THINKS IS...
SHUJIN.
HUH? WHAT, EVEN YOU GET JEALOUS, SAIKO?

I MAY END UP TEAMING UP WITH YOU AFTER ALL.
HUH?
I-IT'S A LITTLE WEIRD TO SUDDENLY HEAR THAT FROM YOU... B-BUT I'M PLEASED...
WE SEEM TO THINK THE SAME, AND I THINK THE STORIES YOU'LL COME UP WITH WILL BE INTERESTING.
AH, IS THAT SO? YOU RECOGNIZE MY SKILLS AT LAST THEN. TOGETHER WE WILL STRIVE FOR THE TOP!!
I SAID "MAY." IF THE STORYBOARD YOU MAKE IS GOOD, THEN I'LL DRAW IT.
HUH? STORYBOARD?
WHAT? YOU'VE BEEN GOING ON AND ON ABOUT HOW IT'S YOUR DREAM TO BECOME A MANGA ARTIST, AND YOU DON'T EVEN KNOW WHAT A STORYBOARD IS?
I DON'T.
DONG DONG
SECOND PERIOD IS STARTING. WILL YOU BE ABLE TO LAST AN HOUR IN CLASS?
YEAH, I'LL TRY.
SO WHAT'S A STORYBOARD?
DO THE RESEARCH YOURSELF, AMATEUR.

I COMPLETELY FLOPPED THE TEST, BUT I STILL MADE IT THROUGH CLASS.
PHEW...
KLAT
DONE FOR THE DAY...
TOO BAD WE HAVE TO GO HOME AND STUDY FOR TOMORROW...
K-LAT
LET'S GO HOME, SAIKO.
SOMETHING'S BEEN BUGGING ME SINCE YOU TOLD ME YOUR UNCLE COMMITTED SUICIDE.
?
WON'T YOUR PARENTS BE AGAINST YOU BECOMING A MANGA ARTIST?
!
I NEVER THOUGHT ABOUT THAT. ACTUALLY, I DIDN'T HAVE ENOUGH ROOM IN MY HEAD TO EVEN THINK ABOUT THAT.
THERE'S NO WAY THEY'LL APPROVE SINCE MY UNCLE DIED THAT WAY...
I'LL GO HOME AND CONVINCE THEM.
ARE YOU SURE? YOUR FACE REALLY DOES LOOK PALE TODAY, YOU KNOW.
YEAH. TOO MANY THINGS ARE HAPPENING ALL AT ONCE, BUT I'VE GOT TO TAKE CARE OF THEM ONE AT A TIME.

THERE IS A RULE AT MY HOUSE.
WHAT IS IT?
WHENEVER I NEED ADVICE OR HAVE SOMETHING I WANT, I TELL MY MOTHER FIRST.
MY MOTHER WILL THEN TELL MY FATHER WHEN I'M NOT AROUND, AND IF HE HAS ANYTHING TO SAY, MY MOTHER WILL THEN TELL ME. IF SHE DOESN'T, THEN THAT MEANS MY FATHER ACCEPTS WHAT I ASKED FOR.
HURRY UP AND TELL ME.
UH...
IN OTHER WORDS, I'VE NEVER REALLY HAD A SERIOUS CONVERSATION WITH MY FATHER.
I'M GOING TO BECOME A MANGA ARTIST.
NO.
THAT WAS FAST.

I'LL GO TO HIGH SCHOOL AND COLLEGE, AND IF I CAN'T PRODUCE RESULTS BEFORE GRADUATING COLLEGE, I'LL GIVE UP.
BUT THAT MEANS YOU'RE GOING TO ATTEND SOME RANDOM SCHOOL AND DRAW MANGA.
YOUR UNCLE MADE HIS DEBUT WHEN HE WAS IN COLLEGE, SO IT'S GOING TO BE THE SAME THING IF I LET YOU DO IT. FORGET ABOUT MANGA AND JUST STUDY MORE.
I KNEW SHE WAS GOING TO BRING UNCLE UP...
!
BUT THAT DOESN'T MEAN I'LL END UP LIKE UNCLE, DOES IT. IT'S NOT LIKE I'M GOING TO COMMIT SUICIDE.
YOU THINK YOUR UNCLE COMMITTED SUICIDE?!
SHOOT, I SHOULDN'T HAVE SAID THAT...
YOUR UNCLE WORKED TOO HARD AND...
YEAH, SORRY. I KNOW. HIS MANGA DIDN'T SELL, AND HE WORKED TOO HARD TO CREATE A POPULAR MANGA... I JUST THOUGHT IT WAS SUICIDE FOR HIM TO KEEP DRAWING UNTIL HE DIED...
BAM
AT ANY RATE, THE ANSWER IS NO. YOUR FATHER WON'T ALLOW IT EITHER.
GOT THAT? END OF CONVERSATION.

Anybody Can Do It
NO MATTER WHAT THEY SAY... EVEN IF THEY DISOWN ME, I'M GOING TO BECOME A MANGA ARTIST.
KADUMP
DAD'S HOME.
TEN MINUTES ... NO, FIVE MINUTES ...?
TMP TMP TMP
THAT WAS FAST. WHICH MEANS DAD GAVE A QUICK ANSWER TOO...
KNOCK KNOCK
MORITAKA, CAN I COME IN?
S-SURE...
I TOLD YOUR FATHER ABOUT IT.
YEAH?

"LET HIM DO IT."
"MEN HAVE DREAMS THAT WOMEN WILL NEVER BE ABLE TO UNDERSTAND."
THAT'S WHAT HE SAID.
FOR SOME REASON, TEARS STARTED TO WELL UP IN MY EYES.
BUT I DIDN'T WANT MY MOTHER TO SEE THEM, SO I HELD THEM BACK.
COME DOWN-STAIRS.
HUH?
TO GRANDPA'S ROOM.
HE'S THE ONE WHO LOST HIS SON TO MANGA, YOU KNOW.
YOU TELL HIM YOUR-SELF.

GRANDPA?
WHAT IS IT, MORITAKA?
I'M GOING TO BECOME A MANGA ARTIST.
HMM, MANGA ARTIST...
YES.
"HMM" ...?
OOOF.
SHF SHF

MORITAKA, TAKE THIS.
JINGLE
KEYS ...?
GRAND-PA!
FATHER... IS THIS YOUR ANSWER?
YUP.
WHAT'RE THOSE KEYS FOR...?
...
THEY'RE THE KEYS TO YOUR UNCLE'S PLACE.
?!

I LEFT NOBUHIRO'S ROOM EXACTLY THE SAME AFTER HE DIED.
YOU CAN HAVE IT.
GR... GRANDPA...
BUT I JUST DECIDED TO BECOME A MANGA ARTIST.
IT'S WAY TOO EARLY FOR ME TO HAVE AN OFFICE...
I KNOW. YOU'RE NOT GOING TO NEED IT FOR SOME TIME STILL, BUT IT WON'T HURT TO BE READY.
THAT PLACE IS PACKED WITH THE THINGS YOU NEED TO BECOME A MANGA ARTIST, ISN'T IT?
SO? DON'T YOU WANT IT?

CAN I GO SEE IT NOW?
DON'T BE ABSURD. IT'S PAST TEN O'CLOCK, AND YOU HAVE A TEST TOMORROW ...
GO.
THANKS.
CHAK
THANK YOU! I'LL GO GET READY.
FATHER ...
IT'S GOOD THAT HE'S BEING THIS WAY.
TRAIN FARE AND MY CELL PHONE...
MORITAKA'S CHANGED. I WAS WORRIED THAT HE'D END UP USELESS...
WHY DID I BUY A KNICKKNACK LIKE THIS? SO STUPID...
DMP

UNCLE'S STUDIO...
IT'S BEEN THREE YEARS...
HELLLOOOO, MY BELOVED SAIKO! ANYTHING NEW GOING ON WITH YOU AND AZUKI...?
I'LL SHOW YOU WHAT A STORYBOARD IS, SO COME MEET ME.
WHAT?
THEY GAVE ME MY UNCLE'S STUDIO!
HUH?
AFTER MY UNCLE DIED, THEY LEFT HIS OFFICE ALONE. AND NOW THEY'RE GIVING IT TO ME!
Y-YOU MEAN YOU TOLD THEM YOU WANTED TO BECOME A MANGA ARTIST, AND THEY GAVE IT TO YOU?
YEAH.
AWESOME!
WHERE ARE YOU NOW?
I'M HEADING FOR KITA-YAKUSA STATION. HIS PLACE IS IN YAKUSA.
OH, THAT'S JUST ONE STATION. I'LL BE THERE IN A MINUTE, SO WAIT FOR ME AT KITA-YAKUSA.
AND THAT'S HOW SHUJIN AND I ENDED UP AT MY UNCLE'S STUDIO THAT NIGHT.

OHBA'S STORYBOARD

OBATA'S STORYBOARD

COMPLETE!

*CREATOR STORYBOARDS AND FINISHED PAGES IN JAPANESE

BAKUMAN。 vol. 1

"Until the Final Draft Is Complete"

Chapter 2, pp. 66-67

CHAPTER 3 PEN AND STORYBOARD
AFTER I TOLD MY PARENTS I WAS GOING TO BECOME A MANGA ARTIST, I HEADED TO MY LATE UNCLE'S OFFICE WITH SHUJIN.
MY GRANDFATHER DECIDED TO GIVE ME THE OFFICE MY UNCLE WAS USING WHEN HE WAS A MANGA ARTIST.
SO IT'S IN THIS COMPLEX, HUH?
YEAH, NINTH FLOOR.
CHAK
KRII...
KLIK
WHOA!

WH... WHAT'S WITH ALL THESE SUPERHERO ACTION FIGURES?
ACTION HERO
MY UNCLE DREW ALL SORTS OF SUPERHERO MANGA, SO HE COLLECTED THESE FIGURES AS PART OF HIS BUSINESS EXPENSES.
FOR GAG SUPERHERO MANGA?
ARE YOU MAKING FUN OF HIM?
NO, I RESPECT HIM.
THEY'RE ALL PACKED IN TIGHT. CAN I PULL ONE OUT AND SEE WHAT'S BEHIND?
OKAY.

ACTION HERO
ACTION HERO
PRODUCED BY
ミラクルマン
CHAPTER 3
PEN AND STORYBOARD
RULER
(MAGAZINES: WEEKLY SHONEN JUMP)
ACTION HERO
ACTION
WHOA, JUMP MAGAZINES
I THINK HE KEPT ALL THE *JUMP* MAGAZINES THAT HAD HIS MANGA IN THEM.
BEHIND THIS DOOR IS THE ACTUAL WORK AREA.
SHHK...
FROM 1996? THAT'S OLD... BUT I WANNA READ THEM LATER.

WOW... IT'S A LOT LARGER THAN I THOUGHT.
IT USED TO BE A THREE-ROOM APARTMENT WITH A DINING AREA AND KITCHEN, BUT HE HAD THE WALL TAKEN DOWN AND MADE IT ALL INTO ONE ROOM.
THE BLEND
114
ink
Zebra

THIS PLACE BRINGS BACK MEMORIES... ESPECIALLY THE SMELL OF CIGARETTES. I CAN'T REMEMBER HOW MANY TIMES I DROPPED BY HERE TO TALK TO HIM...
LOOK AT ALL THESE COMIC BOOKS!
I THOUGHT I HAD A LOT, BUT THIS PLACE HAS LIKE 100 TIMES AS MUCH.
BAM
IT'S THE SAME WITH ALL THE *JUMP* MAGAZINES YOU JUST SAW...
MY UNCLE SAID THE BEST REFERENCE MATERIAL FOR MANGA IS MANGA. THAT MAY JUST BE MY UNCLE THOUGH, SINCE HE WAS NEVER ABLE TO DRAW THAT WELL.
OOH.
H-HEY, THERE SHOULD BE SOME ORIGINAL FINAL DRAFTS HERE, RIGHT? CAN I SEE THEM?
SURE. I THINK THEY'RE INSIDE THAT CLOSET...

ZWAK
Reference Material 3
Final Draft 20
Final Draft 15
Reference Material 2
Final Draft 19
Figures 5
Final Draft 18
THESE BOXES ALL LINE UP SO NEATLY. HE MUST HAVE BEEN A VERY ORGANIZED PERSON.
Reference Material
Figures
DIP PENS...
"MOST PROFESSIONALS USE THIS G-PEN, BUT I CAN'T USE IT, SO I USE A KABURA-PEN.
"I DRAW A GAG MANGA, SO IT'S ALLOWABLE, BUT IF YOU'RE A PROFESSIONAL, YOU SHOULD USE A G-PEN. I'VE GIVEN IT A TRY EVERY NOW AND THEN, BUT IT'S REALLY DIFFICULT."

CAN I REALLY SEE THEM?
YEAH.
I'VE NEVER DRAWN ANYTHING WITH A DIP PEN BEFORE.
THIS IS THE FIRST TIME I'VE LAID EYES ON AN ORIGINAL FINAL DRAFT...
A-AND HERE I THOUGHT YOUR UNCLE WAS BAD AT DRAWING... NOW THAT I'M LOOKING AT THIS DRAFT, I'M STARTING TO WORRY THAT YOU MIGHT NOT BE ABLE TO DO SOMETHING LIKE THIS.
QUESTION NUMBER 3!
WHAT NOW?
I'M NOT SURE ABOUT THAT EITHER.
THE FINAL DRAFTS ARE FUN, BUT YOU NEED TO LOOK AT THESE FIRST, SHUJIN.
FWP
!
THE STORY-BOARDS.

OH... SO THIS IS A STORY-BOARD...
I SAW IT ONCE ON AN AD FOR A MANGA AWARD BEFORE.
IT'S LIKE THE ROUGH DRAFT OF A MANGA.
YOU DRAW THIS FIRST AND SHOW IT TO THE EDITOR. IF THE EDITOR GIVES YOU THE GO-AHEAD, THEN YOU CREATE THE FINAL DRAFT. YOU HAVE TO KEEP RE-DRAWING THE STORYBOARD UNTIL THE EDITOR SAYS IT'S OKAY.
EDITOR
OK!
BUT THE ONLY PEOPLE WHO ARE ALLOWED TO SHOW THEIR STORYBOARD TO THE EDITORS ARE THOSE WHO HAVE BEEN ACCEPTED AS MANGA ARTISTS.
WE HAVE TO START BY SENDING EDITORS A COMPLETE FINAL DRAFT, OR WE HAVE TO TAKE IT TO THEIR OFFICE DIRECTLY AND MAKE THEM ACCEPT US.
YEAH, I KNOW THAT-

WAIT, SAIKO. ARE YOU SAYING I HAVE TO DO THIS?
I CAN'T JUST WRITE THE STORY IN SENTENCES?
OF COURSE NOT.
AND I DID SAY THIS IS A STORYBOARD, BUT YOU CAN'T COPY THIS.
MY UNCLE'S MANGA WAS A GAG MANGA, SO IT WAS OKAY TO HAVE EACH OF THE PANELS SO SMALL. BUT WE CAN'T HAVE TEN PANELS ON A PAGE. BESIDES, THESE PANELS ARE TOO SIMPLISTIC.
YOU HAVE TO CREATE A STORYBOARD THAT FITS YOUR STORY. IF YOU'RE GOING TO JUST GIVE ME A BUNCH OF SENTENCES AND TELL ME THAT'S THE STORY, THEN YOU SHOULD BECOME A NOVELIST OR TEAM UP WITH SOMEBODY ELSE INSTEAD.
I SAID I WON'T TEAM UP WITH YOU IF YOU CAN'T CREATE A STORYBOARD THAT I LIKE.
...
OF COURSE, I'LL RESTRUCTURE THE WHOLE THING WHEN I DRAW IT, AND I'LL FIX A LOT OF THE PANELS TOO.
BUT YOU HAVE TO CREATE SOMETHING THAT WILL CONVINCE ME TO DRAW IT.
SAIKO...
THIS GUY REALLY IS AMAZING...

OKAY, I'LL DO IT! I'LL DO IT FOR YOU!!
I'M STARTING TO GET EXCITED!
SAIKO, WHAT KIND OF MANGA DO YOU WANT TO DRAW?
I DON'T KNOW OFF THE TOP OF MY HEAD...
Final Draft
Final Draft
...BUT I LIKE MANGA THAT'S MANLY.
I DON'T LIKE THE OTAKU KIND OR THOSE ONES WITH WISHY-WASHY STORIES.
YEAH, I DON'T WANT TO DO ANYTHING LIKE THAT EITHER. SEX, RAPE, PREGNANCY, ABORTION... I HATE THOSE THINGS.
THAT STUFF'S IN GIRLS' MANGA AND STUPID ROMANCE NOVELS...
OH, BUT YOU CAN'T FORGET ABOUT INCURABLE ILLNESSES. THAT'S LIKE THE NUMBER ONE TEARJERKER ELEMENT.
YEAH, THAT'S TRUE.
Storyboard (Turned Down)
Final Draft

MANLY MANGA, HUH... WHAT EXACTLY DO YOU MEAN?
LIKE, WHAT'S YOUR FAVORITE MANGA?
TOMORROW'S JOE.
THAT'S SUPER OLD...
BUT IT'S A CLASSIC.
FWSH
I STARTED READING THAT MANGA AFTER WATCHING RERUNS OF THE ANIME. I SERIOUSLY WANTED TO BECOME A BOXER AFTER THAT.
HAHA, YOU'RE AN IDIOT, SHUJIN. BUT I FELT THE SAME WAY.
PUNCH.
PUNCH.
HEH HEH.
HEY, NOW THAT MANGA WAS CREATED BY TWO GENIUSES, DON'T YOU THINK?
FWSH
YEAH, THAT AUTHOR WAS WRITING FIVE STORIES AT THE SAME TIME FOR WEEKLY MAGAZINES.
FOOM
FWSH
WHSH
FWSH
FIVE ?!
WOW... I'M A PRETTY CONFIDENT GUY, BUT I'D NEVER BE ABLE TO DO THAT.

I'VE BEEN READING POPULAR MANGA AND NOVELS THAT I DON'T EVEN LIKE AS RESEARCH THESE DAYS...
...SO MAYBE THAT'S WHY I CAME UP WITH SEX, RAPE, PREGNANCY AND ABORTION.
SHUJIN, I'M STARTING TO THINK THAT YOU'RE GOING TO BE ABLE TO DO IT.
HUH? YOU DO? WHY?
THIS IS ABOUT MY UNCLE AGAIN, BUT HE SUBMITTED HIS WORK FOR THE AKATSUKA AWARD.
SURE, ONE OF THE TWO GREAT MANGA AWARDS. THAT'S THE ONE FOR GAG MANGA.
AKATSUKA AWARD
WHAT HE DID AT THE VERY BEGINNING WAS GATHER TONS OF THAT AWARD'S WINNING PIECES AND ANALYZE THE KIND OF SUBJECTS THAT WERE IN THEM.
HE CAME TO THE CONCLUSION THAT HUMOROUS MANGA WITH SOCIAL SATIRES WERE POPULAR, SO HE CREATED SOMETHING THAT FIT THAT SUBJECT.

SUPER HERO LEGEND
imated Series
AND WAS HE CONSIDERED FOR THE AWARD?
YEAH.
THAT'S KINDA SNEAKY... HE WENT ALL OUT, DIDN'T HE.
WELL, IF YOU SERIOUSLY WANT TO BECOME A MANGA ARTIST, I THINK THAT'S ONE STRATEGY TO USE. AFTER ALL, YOU'RE DOING SOME-THING SIMILAR, SHUJIN.
SO ACCORDING TO YOUR RESEARCH, WHAT KIND OF MANGA ARE POPULAR NOWADAYS?
I DON'T HAVE SOLID RESULTS YET, BUT IN THE CASE OF *JUMP*...
...IT LOOKS LIKE A SPORTS MANGA WITH SWEAT AND GUTS ISN'T GOING TO BE VERY POPULAR, UNFORTUNATELY.
...
IT'S JUST A SIGN OF THE TIMES, I GUESS. IT'D BE IMPRESSIVE IF WE COULD ACTUALLY BECOME NUMBER ONE WITH THAT TYPE OF MANGA NOW...
...BUT I DON'T KNOW ANY SPORT WELL ENOUGH TO WRITE ABOUT IT...
VSH
I JUST SAID I LIKED *JOE*. I DIDN'T MEAN WE HAVE TO DO A SPORTS MANGA.
I DID FIND ONE COMMONALITY IN MANY OF THE POPULAR MANGA THOUGH.
!

SWORDS.
NARUTO, ONE PIECE, BLEACH, GIN TAMA...
THERE ARE TONS OF OTHER MANGA WITH SWORDS AND BLADES IN THEM TOO.
THEY USUALLY HAVE BATTLES, AND THEY'RE ALL SET IN A DIFFERENT WORLD.
VSH
I DON'T REALLY WANT TO PUT SWORDS IN THE STORY JUST BECAUSE THEY'RE POPULAR...
...BUT I HAVE TO ADMIT THAT I NEVER NOTICED THAT BEFORE... THERE SURE ARE A LOT OF SWORDS, HUH.
NOT NOTICING THAT CHARACTERISTIC ISN'T A PROBLEM. I MEAN, NOBODY REALLY ANALYZES MANGA AS THEY'RE READING IT.
(MANGA: BEET THE VANDAL BUSTER ON THE LEFT AND DRAGON BALL ON THE RIGHT)
HEY, WHAT'S YOUR FAVORITE MANGA, SHUJIN?
CHOOSING A FAVORITE IS HARD, BUT...
...I'D HAVE TO SAY IT'S DRAGON BALL.
YOUR FAVORITE MANGA ISN'T EXACTLY NEW EITHER, YOU KNOW.

I GUESS I LIKE MANGA DRAWN BY GENIUSES.
DOES THAT MEAN ONLY GENIUSES CAN CREATE GOOD MANGA AFTER ALL?
WELL, WHAT'S THE BEST MANGA DRAWN BY A NON-GENIUS?
THE GREATEST ONE-HIT WONDER IN HISTORY, HUH...
NAH. YOU'D STILL BE CONSIDERED A GENIUS IF YOU CAN LIVE OFF OF A ONE-HIT WONDER SERIES FOR THE REST OF YOUR LIFE.
HMM... THAT'S DIFFICULT.
ANYWAY, IT'S POINTLESS FOR US TO FIGURE THAT OUT. WE'RE TRYING TO BE GENIUSES OURSELVES, AREN'T WE?
YEAH...
HEY, I'M GONNA LOOK AT AS MANY STORYBOARDS AS I CAN TODAY BEFORE GOING HOME.

SAIKO... YOU SAID I CAN'T JUST COPY THESE...
...BUT THESE ARE GREAT REFERENCES. ESPECIALLY THESE PROOF COMMENTS IN RED.
FLLP
IS IT OKAY IF I TAKE THESE HOME WITH ME?
IT'S FINE AS LONG AS YOU BRING THEM BACK.
WHOA, SERIOUSLY? HOW MANY BOXES CAN I TAKE HOME WITH ME? THEY'RE PRETTY HEAVY...
SHUJIN IS REALLY GETTING INTO THIS.
I'M SURE HE'LL BE ABLE TO COME UP WITH AN INTERESTING STORY AND CREATE A STORYBOARD FOR IT.
BUT I'VE NEVER DRAWN ANYTHING WITH A DIP PEN BEFORE...
...SO HOW LONG IS IT GOING TO TAKE ME TO GET USED TO THAT?
SHUJIN.
WHAT?
DO YOU THINK WE'LL BE ABLE TO GET OUR MANGA ANIMATED BY THE TIME WE'RE 18 YEARS OLD?
NOPE.

Japanese Spirit
Final Draft (41)
Final Draft (40)
Reference Material (7)
Figures (10)
Storyboard (31)
Storyboard (3)
THAT WAS SO COLD.
YOU KNOW, VOICE ACTORS ARE JUST LIKE IDOLS. THEY MAKE THEIR DEBUT AROUND 18.
YEAH, A LOT OF THE VOICE ACTRESSES ARE LIKE THAT THESE DAYS. SOME ARE EVEN YOUNGER THAN 18...
!
OH.
YEAH.
AZUKI'S CUTE, SO THERE'S A POSSIBILITY SHE'LL MAKE HER DEBUT BEFORE SHE'S GOOD ENOUGH.
...
SAIKO ...
I ASKED YOU TO TEAM UP WITH ME BECAUSE I WANTED TO BECOME A MANGA CREATOR.
BUT NOW, I WANT YOU AND AZUKI TO GET MARRIED JUST AS MUCH. I'M NOT LYING.
Storyboard

I KNOW. LET'S TRY TO GET OUR MANGA ANIMATED BY THE TIME WE'RE 18 YEARS OLD—NO, WE'LL HAVE TO MAKE THAT HAPPEN!
SHUJIN...
WE'RE GONNA DO IT! I PROMISE YOU!
HEY, SAIKO. WHERE'S THE STORYBOARD FOR THIS FINAL DRAFT? I WANT TO COMPARE THEM.
OH, IT SHOULD BE IN ONE OF THESE BOXES.
OKAY, I'LL LOOK FOR IT.
TMP TMP TMP
I'LL HELP YOU.
FWF
THANKS.
HOW MANY STORYBOARDS ARE THERE? EVERY BOX IS PACKED WITH THEM...
OH, I'VE READ THIS ONE BEFORE. I THINK IT WAS A ONE-SHOT...

AND THERE'S STILL MORE LEFT INSIDE THE CLOSET...
THE ONES THAT WERE MADE INTO A FINAL DRAFT ARE PROBABLY LIKE A TENTH... NO, A HUNDREDTH OF ALL THIS... HOW MUCH DID HE HAVE TO DRAW TO CREATE SO MUCH...?
...
SO MUCH...
I'M GOING OUT TO MAKE A PHONE CALL.
AZUKI?
I DON'T KNOW HER PHONE NUMBER...

HI, DAD.
WHAT'S WRONG? THIS IS THE FIRST TIME YOU'VE EVER CALLED ME...
SORRY. ALL THIS TIME, I THOUGHT UNCLE COMMITTED SUICIDE.
BUT THE TRUTH IS HE HARDLY SLEPT...
DON'T BE STUPID. YOUR UNCLE WASN'T A GUTLESS COWARD WHO'D THINK ABOUT KILLING HIMSELF. HE'S THE KIND OF GUY WHO'D GNASH HIS TEETH AND KEEP DOING HIS BEST NO MATTER HOW TOUGH THE SITUATION GOT... WITHOUT EVEN COMPLAINING ABOUT IT.
YEAH. I REMEMBER NOW. NO MATTER WHEN I WENT TO SEE HIM, HE WAS ALWAYS DRAWING SOMETHING QUIETLY.
MORITAKA, HAVE YOU READ THE MANGA *STAR OF THE GIANTS*?
HUH? YEAH.
THEN YOU KNOW THAT RYOMA SAKAMOTO PHRASE, DON'T YOU?
UH-HUH.

I REMEMBER YOU LIKED TOMORROW'S JOE.
UH-HUH...
THANKS, DAD. YOU DON'T HAVE TO SAY ANYTHING ELSE.
OKAY. I'M HANGING UP THEN.
KLAK
RYOMA SAKAMOTO'S PHRASE... "IF YOU ARE A MAN, PLUNGE FORWARD AS YOU DIE. EVEN IF YOU ARE DYING IN THE GUTTERS."
AS FOR JOE YABUKI, HE GAVE ALL HE COULD AND BURNT INTO WHITE ASH...
MY UNCLE PLUNGED FORWARD INTO DEATH AND BURNT INTO WHITE ASH...
MY DAD TRIED TO TELL ME WHAT I SHOULD DO AS A MAN USING FAMOUS PHRASES FROM MANGA...
I'M NOT GOING TO DO THIS HALF-HEARTEDLY.
MANGA... MIHO AZUKI... I'M GOING TO POUR MY LIFE INTO THIS.

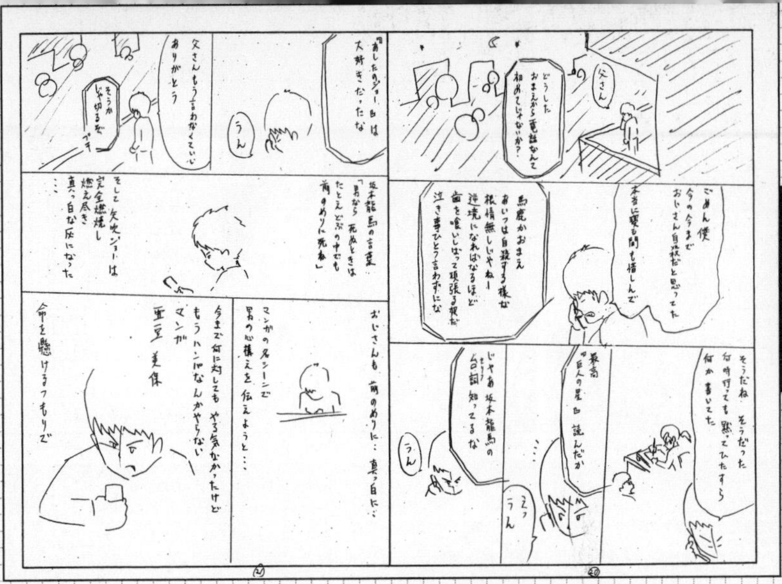

OHBA'S STORYBOARD

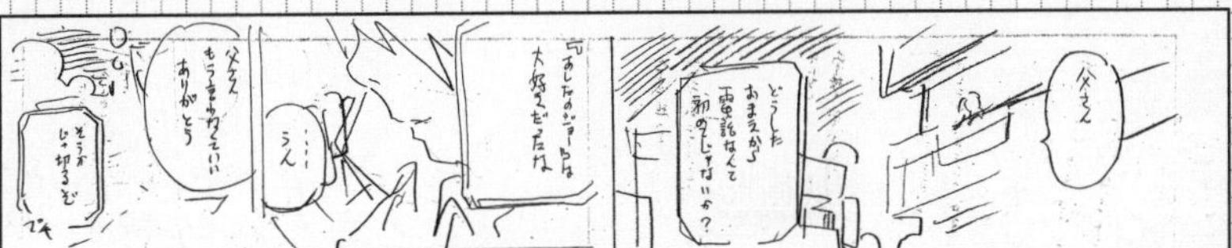

OBATA'S STORYBOARD

COMPLETE!

*CREATOR STORYBOARDS AND FINISHED PAGES IN JAPANESE

BAKUMAN。 vol.1

"Until the Final Draft Is Complete"

Chapter 3, pp. 116-117

AFTER MY GRANDFATHER GAVE ME MY UNCLE'S STUDIO, SHUJIN AND I WERE RUMMAGING THROUGH ALL THE STORYBOARDS AND FINAL DRAFTS THERE.
THIS ONE IS SO FUN... I DON'T UNDERSTAND WHY THEY TURNED IT DOWN.
DON'T STEAL THE IDEA.
I HAVE NO INTENTION OF CREATING A GAG MANGA.
CHAPTER 4 PARENT AND CHILD
HOW MANY REJECTED STORYBOARDS ARE THERE, ANYWAY?
EVERY BOX WAS LABELED WITH "FINAL DRAFT," "STORY-BOARD," OR "REFERENCE MATERIAL"...
Reference Material (16)
Storyboard (Rejected)
?!
...BUT THERE WAS THIS ONE STRANGE-LOOKING BOX AMONG THEM.
SHOOT, I BET IT'S GOT DIRTY DVDS INSIDE.

LETTERS...
To: Nobuhiro Mashiro
To: Nobuhiro Mashiro
"WE WENT TO DIFFERENT HIGH SCHOOLS, SO WE NEVER SAW EACH OTHER. BUT WE KEPT SENDING EACH OTHER LETTERS WITH THINGS LIKE 'HOW ARE YOU DOING?' AND 'GOOD LUCK.' YOU KNOW, THAT SORT OF THING."
THIS IS...
SHK
Dear Mashiro,
How are you doing?
I've finally started getting
used to high school.
My class is, to put it in simple
terms, like that old TV drama
"The Rise of Youth"? Do I have
the title right? It's the kind of
class where everybody's a bit
noisy, but it's a very nice and
cheerful class. I've made some
and enjoying it here
one day

CHAPTER 4
PARENT AND CHILD

WHAT'S UP, SAIKO?
MY UNCLE WAS IN LOVE WITH THIS WOMAN, AND THEY WERE EXCHANGING LETTERS FOR A LONG TIME.
EXCHANGING LETTERS? HOW OLD SCHOOL... SO THEY LIVED FAR AWAY FROM EACH OTHER, HUH.
NO, THEY LIVED IN THE SAME CITY.
HUH? LEMME SEE THAT.
SHFF
"I WENT TO THE ALFEE CONCERT, AND I FEEL LIKE I'VE BECOME A LITTLE MORE ACTIVE THAN I WAS IN MIDDLE SCHOOL"...
"I'VE NEVER LIKED THE RAINY SEASON, BUT AFTER I BOUGHT TWO NEW UMBRELLAS, I'VE STARTED TO LIKE IT"... THIS IS JUST SOME REALLY RANDOM, **MUNDANE** STUFF.
THEY PROBABLY COULDN'T WRITE ABOUT THEIR FEELINGS EVEN THOUGH THEY LOVED EACH OTHER.
HUH? I DON'T GET WHAT YOU MEAN.
MY UNCLE SAID HE COULDN'T TELL HER HIS FEELINGS WHILE HE WAS STILL A GAMBLER... HE HAD TO BECOME A REAL MANGA ARTIST FIRST.
AH... I UNDERSTAND.

THE LETTERS WERE ORGANIZED IN THE ORDER THEY CAME.
"CONGRATULATIONS ON RECEIVING HONORABLE MENTION FOR THE AKATSUKA AWARD"... SO THIS IS WHEN HE GOT THAT.
YOU CAN REALLY SEE WHAT KIND OF LIVES THESE TWO WERE HAVING.
WE FELT BAD FOR READING THESE LETTERS FROM MIYUKI HARUNO, BUT WE COULDN'T STOP. I COULD SENSE THE DELICATE RELATIONSHIP BETWEEN THE TWO OF THEM, AND EVEN I FELT FRUSTRATED ABOUT IT.
AND THIS IS THE LAST LETTER.
YEAH.
KRNK
I haven't been able to tell you, but I'm going to get married next spring. That's why I'll only be able to keep writing to you until that day comes. I know I sound selfish, but you understand, don't you?
It brings me great joy knowing that we've been able to exchange letters for over ten years ever since we graduated middle school. I felt so happy every time I received a letter from you. It didn't matter what you wrote.
able
married
able
day
WHA... WHAT IS THIS...? SHE NEVER WROTE ABOUT HAVING A BOYFRIEND, SO THIS IS SO OUT OF THE BLUE.

I WONDER HOW MY UNCLE FELT WHEN HE WAS READING THIS...
SINCE THIS IS THE LAST LETTER, IT MUST MEAN HE STOPPED WRITING TO HER AFTER THIS.
WHEN DID SUPER-HERO LEGEND START?
UM, IT SHOULD SAY ON THE COMIC BOOK...
room filled
smoke from the
Am I up in the clouds?
I feel like an angel!
Then I got a phone call and
was dragged back to reality.
I really am a manga artist...
Ha ha ha.
●Serialized in Weekly Shonen Jump 1995 Issue 20 - 1995, Issue 30.
LOVE
YEAR 1995, ISSUE 20... SO THAT'S AROUND THE SPRING OF 1995.
SO THAT WAS TWO YEARS AFTER HE GOT THIS LETTER...
AND IT WOULD BE ANOTHER TWO YEARS BEFORE THIS SERIES TURNED INTO AN ANIME.
HE DIDN'T MAKE IT IN TIME... I'M SURPRISED HE DIDN'T GIVE UP AND ACTUALLY WENT SO FAR. WILLPOWER... NO, MAYBE MORE LIKE OBSESSION...
...
"HOWEVER, I'VE BEEN ABLE TO COME THIS FAR BECAUSE SHE WAS AROUND. I CAN CONTINUE DRAWING MANGA WITHOUT GIVING UP BECAUSE I STILL BELIEVE THAT SHE'S WATCHING ME."

HEY... WHAT'S THAT?
HM?
Final Draft 38
THERE'S SOMETHING IN THAT BOX STILL.
OH?
Yakusa City Municipal Meiyo Middle
YEARBOOK
YOUR UNCLE COULDN'T EVEN ASK HER FOR A PICTURE.
HOW PURE-HEARTED WAS HE?
EVEN PEOPLE IN THE TAISHO ERA WERE MORE AGGRESSIVE THAN HE WAS.
AAAH!
...
OH GEEZ!
MIYUKI HARUNO! LOOK FOR MIYUKI!!
I KNOW, I KNOW. PIPE DOWN, I'M LOOKING FOR HER RIGHT NOW.
FWP
FWP

WHAT...
AZUKI...?
Yakusa City Municipal Me
YEARB
AH...
IT'S AZUKI'S MOM!
SHE'S AZUKI'S MOTHER!!
...

I KNEW IT! IT'S IN THE BLOOD! THE DNA, THE DNA! WHOA, DNA IS SO FREAKY...
AND YOU'RE UNBELIEVABLY PUREHEARTED LIKE YOUR UNCLE TOO.
THE WHOLE IDEA OF ENCOURAGING EACH OTHER THROUGH LETTERS AND EMAIL MESSAGES IS COMPLETELY THE SAME.
BUT I CAN'T BELIEVE HOW MUCH THEY LOOK ALIKE! SHE MAY BE HER MOTHER, BUT STILL... DNA IS SO FREAKY!
...
WE STILL DON'T KNOW THAT SHE'S AZUKI'S MOTHER, DO WE?
I KNOW SHE IS. BUT LET'S GO FIND OUT FOR SURE.
FIND OUT, HOW?
WE'LL DROP BY AZUKI'S HOUSE AGAIN AND ASK HER MOTHER POINT BLANK.
WHAT?!
TOMORROW... WELL, TODAY, TO BE EXACT. EVERY WEDNESDAY, AZUKI HAS DANCE PRACTICE FROM 5 TO 7, SO WE'LL GO DURING THAT TIME.
HMM... SO AZUKI IS LEARNING HOW TO DANCE. I GUESS VOICE ACTRESSES NOWADAYS HAVE TO BE ABLE TO DANCE TOO...?
WHY DON'T YOU JUST ASK AZUKI WHAT HER MOTHER'S MAIDEN NAME IS?
BUT WE'LL ONLY BE ABLE CONFIRM WHETHER OR NOT IT'S HER MOTHER.

THERE ARE TONS OF OTHER THINGS YOU WANT TO ASK HER, RIGHT?
YOU JUST WANT TO DO THIS FOR THE FUN OF IT, DON'T YOU?
RIIING...
AZUKI?
FLP
I TOLD YOU WE DON'T HAVE EACH OTHER'S CELL PHONE NUMBERS!
SHOOT, IT'S MY MOM.
DO YOU HAVE ANY IDEA WHAT TIME IT IS? QUIT WHAT YOU'RE DOING, AND COME HOME THIS INSTANT!
OKAY, I'M HEADING BACK.
C'MON, LET'S GO TO AZUKI'S HOUSE TODAY.
WHY DON'T YOU GO BY YOURSELF?
IT WAS PAST 2 A.M. THE TRAINS HAD STOPPED RUNNING, SO SHUJIN AND I TOOK ABOUT AN HOUR TO WALK HOME.

OBVIOUSLY, I COMPLETELY CRASHED AND BURNED DURING THE SECOND DAY OF MIDTERMS.
IF AZUKI'S MOTHER WAS REALLY THE PERSON MY UNCLE WAS IN LOVE WITH...
...THEN THERE'S SOME-THING I HAVE TO FIND OUT ABOUT...
DONG
DONG
DONG
KLAT
KLAT
FINE, LET'S GO TO AZUKI'S HOUSE.
AH-HA.
I KNEW YOU'D WANT TO ASK MORE ABOUT THEIR RELATIONSHIP.
IT'S NOT THAT.

...
KLIK
SHAA
OKAY, NOW.
I FEEL LIKE WE'RE STALKING HER.
I FEEL LIKE A DETECTIVE, SO THIS IS FUN! LIKE I'M GEVANNI FROM *DEATH NOTE*.
DING DONG
YOU DIDN'T PAUSE BEFORE PRESSING THE DOORBELL TODAY.
EVERYTHING'S EASIER THE SECOND TIME AROUND.
YES?
I'M AKITO TAKAGI, MIHO'S CLASSMATE.
AGAIN YOU FORGET TO TELL HER THAT I'M HERE TOO...

AZUKI
I'M SORRY, MIHO'S OUT RIGHT NOW. IF THERE'S ANYTHING YOU WANT ME TO TELL HER...
ACTUALLY, WE'RE HERE TO SEE YOU TODAY.
ME?
ABOUT THE MANGA ARTIST TARO KAWAGUCHI...
...
WE... MORITAKA MASHIRO AND I ARE TRYING TO BECOME MANGA CREATORS TOO.
...
...
THIS RESPONSE... SHE REALLY MUST BE THE WOMAN MY UNCLE WAS IN LOVE WITH.
IT'S SO NICE TO BE YOUNG... ALL RIGHT, COME ON IN. I'LL MAKE YOU SOME TEA.
YES!

COME IN.
WHOA, SHE LOOKS LIKE AZUKI. REALLY BEAUTIFUL... LET'S SEE, SHE'S THE SAME AGE AS MY UNCLE, WHO'S TWO YEARS YOUNGER THAN MY DAD, SO THAT MAKES HER... 42...? WOW, 42-YEAR-OLDS LOOK SO YOUNG THESE DAYS! MAYBE THIS IS WHAT AZUKI WILL LOOK LIKE 28 YEARS FROM NOW? NOT BAD AT ALL. BUT I DON'T THINK I WANT HER TO CURL HER HAIR LIKE THAT.
SIT ANYWHERE YOU LIKE. I'LL GO MAKE SOME TEA.
OH, THANK YOU.
SO THIS IS THE LIVING ROOM WHERE AZUKI SPENDS HER TIME EVERY DAY...
I FEEL KINDA NERVOUS ABOUT BEING HERE...

YOU'RE NOBUHIRO MASHIRO'S OLDER BROTHER'S SON, RIGHT?
OH, YES.
SO SHE KNOWS.
YOUR FATHER WAS TWO YEARS ABOVE ME IN MIDDLE SCHOOL, AND HE WAS THE CAPTAIN OF THE JUDO TEAM. HE WAS PRETTY WELL KNOWN FOR BEING A HARD WORKER...
OH, YEAH. MY DAD OFTEN COMPLAINS THAT YOUNG GUYS THESE DAYS DON'T HAVE WILL-POWER.
LET'S SEE... BLACK TEA, COFFEE ...
...OOLONG TEA, COKE, ORANGE JUICE, WINE, BEER... WHAT WOULD YOU LIKE?
OH, COFFEE FOR ME, THANKS.
AREN'T YOU BEING A LITTLE TOO FAMILIAR, SHUJIN? AND SHOULDN'T WE BE TELLING HER THAT WE CAN'T DRINK ALCOHOL?
I'LL HAVE COFFEE TOO THEN.
YOUR UNCLE...
HE OFTEN WROTE IN HIS LETTERS THAT HE ALWAYS DRANK BLACK COFFEE WHEN HE WAS WORKING.
HUH. THE FORMER SECRETARY IN HER JUST COUGHED UP EVIDENCE THAT SHE'S THE ONE MY UNCLE SENT LETTERS TO BEFORE WE EVEN ASKED HER ABOUT IT.
OKAY... ASK AWAY, BOYS.
KLINK

WELL, WE ALREADY KNOW THAT YOU'RE THE PERSON MASHIRO'S UNCLE HAD A CRUSH ON, SO...
HEY, BEFORE THAT...
SORRY, WE READ ALL THE LETTERS YOU SENT HIM.
BOW
WE'RE REALLY SORRY.
BOW
WHAT?
MY, THAT'S EMBAR-RASSING.
EVERY SINGLE ONE OF THEM?
YES.
A WOMAN AT HER AGE BLUSHING...
THAT'S ADORABLE.

I DIDN'T WRITE ANYTHING TOO EMBARRASSING IN THOSE LETTERS...
RIGHT?
R...RIGHT. THE CONTENT WAS UNBELIEVABLY REFRESHING, ACTUALLY.
I SEE. SO HE KEPT ALL MY LETTERS, HUH...
AND YOU READ THEM ALL...
WELL, WHAT'S PAST IS PAST. I FORGIVE YOU.
THANK YOU VERY MUCH.
UM, THOSE LETTERS WERE VERY REFRESHING... AND THEY DIDN'T HAVE ANYTHING SPECIFIC WRITTEN IN THEM...
...BUT YOU WERE IN LOVE WITH HIM, WEREN'T YOU?
HEY, YOU'RE ASKING TOO MUCH.
YES, I DID LOVE HIM.

THEN WHY DIDN'T YOU WRITE THAT IN THE LETTERS?
I COULDN'T DO IT. I WAS TOO EMBARRASSED, AND I ALSO FELT LIKE I SHOULDN'T.
AND ANYWAY, I ALWAYS THOUGHT THAT MEN SHOULD BE THE ONES MAKING THE MOVE.
MAYBE WE WERE BOTH WAITING FOR EACH OTHER TO SAY, "I LOVE YOU"...
...BUT IT TURNED OUT I GOT TIRED OF WAITING. I FELL IN LOVE WITH SOMEONE ELSE AND GOT MARRIED.
WHEN MIHO WAS THREE YEARS OLD, I TURNED ON THE TV AND SAW THE ANIMATED VERSION OF TARO KAWAGUCHI'S MANGA.
WHAT A SHOCK THAT WAS!
I WAS REALLY HAPPY TO KNOW HE WAS WORKING HARD AND DOING WELL.
AFTER THAT, I'D DROP BY THE CONVENIENCE STORE JUST TO READ *SUPER-HERO LEGEND*... EVEN THOUGH IT WAS A BIT EMBARRASSING.
WOW...

THERE WAS A STORYLINE WITH A HERO CALLED ROMANTICIST MAN, AND READING IT BROUGHT TEARS TO MY EYES.
IT SHOWED ME HOW MASHIRO HAD FELT...
!
ROMANTICIST MAN...
AN ABSOLUTE NO-GOOD HERO WHO FALLS IN LOVE WITH A PRINCESS. HE STRIVES TO BECOME THE GREATEST HERO IN THE GALAXY SO THAT HE CAN INVITE HER TO HIS INAUGURATION PARTY AND TELL HER HIS FEELINGS.
BUT BEFORE HE'S ABLE TO BECOME A GREAT HERO, THE PRINCESS GOES TO SEE HIM TO TELL HIM HER FEELINGS.
HE SAYS, "YOU'RE NOT SUPPOSED TO BE HERE. YOU'VE GOTTA WAIT UNTIL I BECOME THE GREATEST IN THE GALAXY. GO BACK TO WHERE YOU BELONG!" HE ENDS UP GETTING SLAPPED IN THE FACE.
HYUU
CRASH
SHLAP

SO THAT STORY WAS A MESSAGE TO YOU.
THAT'S HOW I TOOK IT.
WELL DONE, TARO KAWAGUCHI.
NOW, CAN I ASK YOU TWO A QUESTION?
YES?
TAKAGI AND MASHIRO...
WHICH ONE OF YOU IS GOING OUT WITH MIHO?
OH, NEITHER OF US ARE AT THIS POINT. BUT HE'LL BE GOING OUT WITH HER IN THE FUTURE.
HEY!
I'M GLAD TO HEAR THAT.
?

I'VE NEVER BEEN TOO FOND OF MEN WHO ARE EXTREMELY SMART.
FWMP
GIRLS TEND TO LIKE BOYS WHO ARE A LITTLE BAD, YOU KNOW.
BUT THAT'S JUST YOUR TASTE, MRS. AZUKI. THAT'S NOT HOW EVERY GIRL FEELS.
I'M REALLY POPULAR TOO, YOU KNOW... WITH GIRLS WHO ARE OVERLY SERIOUS...
And I'm a bad boy at heart.
DON'T TAKE IT SO PERSONALLY.
Sit down.
HA HA HA. I SEE. I'M SORRY.
HA HA HA...
THAT'S OKAY.
UM...
MIHO DOESN'T KNOW THAT YOU AND MY UNCLE WENT TO SCHOOL TOGETHER...
...AND THAT MY UNCLE HAPPENED TO BE A MANGA ARTIST, DOES SHE?
NO, SHE DOESN'T.
THANK GOODNESS...

NO MATTER WHAT HAPPENS, PLEASE DON'T TELL HER ABOUT THAT.
ALL RIGHT, I'LL NEVER TELL HER.
YOU MUSTN'T TELL HER EITHER, TAKAGI.
POINT
OH, OF COURSE.
SHU
YES?
AKITO TAKAGI.
MORITAKA MASHIRO.
I HOPE YOU BOTH BECOME FINE MANGA ARTISTS. I'LL BE CHEERING FOR YOU TWO FROM THE SIDELINES.
THANK YOU VERY MUCH.
YES!

WE ENDED UP TALKING WITH HER UNTIL JUST MOMENTS BEFORE AZUKI CAME HOME.
I WONDER IF AZUKI WILL TALK THAT MUCH WHEN SHE GROWS UP...
SHE WAS REALLY NICE... AND VERY PRETTY TOO.
I CAN UNDERSTAND WHY YOUR UNCLE FELL IN LOVE WITH HER.
HE WAS ONE HECK OF A ROMANTIC, WASN'T HE. A REAL ROMANTICIST MAN.
MEN'S ROMANTICISM, HUH...
...
YEAH, IT'S A ROMANTIC IDEA FOR A MAN TO DREAM ABOUT BECOMING A MANGA ARTIST, RIGHT?
HEY, WE'RE REALLY BLESSED, YOU KNOW.
EVERYONE'S SUPPORTING US.
AND IT FEELS LIKE FATE THE WAY THE WOMAN YOUR UNCLE WAS IN LOVE WITH TURNS OUT TO BE AZUKI'S MOTHER.

I'M REALLY GOING TO MAKE THIS DREAM COME TRUE!
NOT "I" BUT "WE."
I ADMIT THAT I'M BLESSED.
WOOSH
IT'S "WE."
IT *IS* LIKE FATE HOW AZUKI'S MOTHER IS THE WOMAN MY UNCLE WAS IN LOVE WITH...
...BUT I THINK MY DAD AND GRANDFATHER ALL KNEW HOW MUCH I ADMIRED MY UNCLE WHEN I WAS IN ELEMENTARY SCHOOL.
AFTER ALL, MY GRANDFATHER LEFT THAT WORKPLACE UNTOUCHED...
AND MY DAD DIDN'T OBJECT TO MY IDEA OF BECOMING A MANGA ARTIST...

MY DAD GAVE ME THE GO-AHEAD REALLY QUICKLY, AND MY GRANDFATHER GAVE ME THE STUDIO...
RIGHT. IT'S AS IF THEY KNEW... NO, THEY *WANTED* THIS TO HAPPEN!
I WANT TO MARRY AZUKI, BUT THAT'S NOT THE ONLY REASON I WANT TO BECOME A MANGA ARTIST NOW.
I'M NOT A MAN IF I DON'T BECOME A MANGA ARTIST AFTER ALL THIS...
SHOO
TMP
I'M NOT A MAN IF I DON'T GO FOR IT.
I'M GOING TO START PRACTICING HOW TO DRAW MANGA-STYLE STARTING TOMORROW... NO, TODAY!
OKAY! I'LL START MAKING A STORY-BOARD!!

OHBA'S STORYBOARD

OBATA'S STORYBOARD

COMPLETE!

*CREATOR STORYBOARDS AND FINISHED PAGES IN JAPANESE

BAKUMAN。vol.1

"Until the Final Draft Is Complete"

Chapter 4, pp. 132-133

...
MASHIRO.
MASHIRO, WAKE UP!
HUH?
CHAPTER 5 TIME AND KEY
BANG
TWITCH
CRAP! I FELL ASLEEP DURING THE EXAM!
AH HA HA HA HA HA HA
HA HA HA HA HA
ARE YOU OKAY? YOU'RE THE FIRST GUY I'VE EVER SEEN COMPLETELY FALL ASLEEP DURING A MIDTERM EXAM.
SIGH... I BET AZUKI AND ALL THE OTHERS THOUGHT I MUST HAVE STUDIED REAL HARD FOR THE EXAM...
THEY'RE GOING TO THINK I'M AN ABSOLUTE IDIOT ONCE THEY FIND OUT I COMPLETELY FAILED IT.

WOB... WOB...
SO YOU REALLY DID PRACTICE ALL NIGHT...
YEAH. I PRACTICED 'TIL AFTER MIDNIGHT AT THE STUDIO...
THEN MY MOM CALLED ME, SO I WENT HOME AND PRACTICED 'TIL I CAME TO SCHOOL THIS MORNING.
VSH
CHAPTER 5 TIME AND KEY
FRENCH CURVE
IF I HADN'T CLEARED MY HEAD A BIT DURING MY WALK TO SCHOOL, I PROBABLY WOULD'VE TAKEN THE TEST WITH THIS PEN.
THEN AGAIN, IF I HAD BEEN USING THIS PEN, I PROBABLY WOULDN'T HAVE FALLEN ASLEEP...
WOW...
HE ACTUALLY BROUGHT IT WITH HIM...
I'M NOT GOING ANYWHERE UNTIL I GET USED TO DRAWING WITH THIS.
THERE'RE NO LIMITS WITH MANGA, YOU KNOW.
NO LIMITS?

IT'S DIFFERENT FROM HOW IT IS WITH EXAMS... THERE ARE NO RIGHT ANSWERS. THERE'S NO CAP ON WHAT YOU CAN DRAW OR WHAT THE STORY IS.
THE BETTER YOU GET, THE BETTER IT IS.
RIGHT.
THIS IS THE FIRST TIME I EVER THOUGHT I DIDN'T HAVE ANY TIME TO WASTE... IT'S ALSO THE FIRST TIME I'VE DEDICATED MYSELF TO SOMETHING SO SERIOUSLY.
...
I'M GOING STRAIGHT TO THE STUDIO. DO YOU WANT TO COME TOO?
JINGLE
YEAH!
YOU LOOK HAPPY, SHUJIN.
KLNK
HERE'S A SPARE KEY FOR YOU.
C... CAN I REALLY HAVE IT?
YOU WANT TO DROP BY THE STUDIO WHENEVER YOU WANT TO TOO, RIGHT?
THANKS.

WOW! YOU'VE REALLY GOT DRAWING TALENT, SAIKO! JUST ONE DAY, AND YOU'VE ALREADY DRAWN ALL THESE ILLUSTRATIONS FOR MANGA!
THOSE ARE NO GOOD.
WHY?
THE LINES ARE STIFF, PLUS THEIR WIDTH IS ALL MESSED UP TOO. THEY'RE NOT GOOD ENOUGH FOR MANGA.
Y... YOU THINK SO?
THEY LOOK OKAY TO ME... IN FACT, I THINK HE'S BETTER THAN SOME OF THOSE MANGA ARTISTS WHO AREN'T VERY GOOD DRAWERS.
USING A G-PEN REALLY IS DIFFICULT...
CHAK

I CAN'T DRAW THE LINES IN THE THICKNESS I WANT.
WHAT HE SAID ABOUT THERE BEING NO LIMITS TO MANGA... AT THIS RATE, SAIKO IS GOING TO BECOME AN EXCEPTIONAL MANGA ARTIST.
IT WAS SO HARD, I TRIED USING THE KABURA PEN INSTEAD.
CHAK... CHAK
HUH? KABURA PEN?
THIS ONE.
OH, I ALWAYS THOUGHT THOSE ARE WHAT YOU CALL A DIP PEN. IT'S THE MOST STANDARD KIND, RIGHT?
MY UNCLE DIDN'T KNOW ABOUT G-PENS AND WAS USING THIS KIND UNTIL AN EDITOR TOLD HIM TO USE THE G-PEN. HE GAVE IT A TRY, BUT HE'D GOTTEN SO USED TO USING THIS PEN THAT HE JUST ENDED UP USING IT ALL THE TIME.
IT'S HARD TO DRAW LINES WITH DIFFERENT THICKNESSES WITH THIS PEN, BUT IT'S A LOT EASIER TO DRAW LINES OF EQUAL THICKNESS CONSISTENTLY.
SHUU—

CAN'T YOU JUST USE THIS PEN TOO SINCE YOUR UNCLE USED IT AS A PROFESSIONAL MANGA ARTIST?
OF COURSE NOT. THERE'S NO FLAVOR OR FEELING IN ILLUSTRATIONS DRAWN WITH THIS TYPE OF PEN.
MY UNCLE USED THIS BECAUSE HE JUST DEFIANTLY SAID, "I'M A BAD DRAWER." PLUS HE WORKED ON GAG MANGA, AND IT WAS BARELY OKAY IN HIS CASE.
KLNK
RIGHT...
IT'S TOTALLY DIFFERENT FROM SKETCHING WITH A PENCIL OR DOING A WATERCOLOR PAINTING WITH A BRUSH. I'LL JUST HAVE TO DRAW WITH IT UNTIL I GET USED TO IT.
Ugh.
SINCE I DON'T HAVE ANY ASSISTANTS TO HELP ME, I'VE GOT TO DRAW THE BACKGROUNDS AND EFFECTS MYSELF.
SHA...
SHUNK
I DREW THOSE YESTERDAY TOO.
AMAZING!
BUT I SHOULDN'T SAY THAT SINCE HE'S PROBABLY NOT SATISFIED WITH THEM.
I CAN DRAW THE BACKGROUNDS BETTER WITH A KABURA PEN. THE REALLY THIN LINES I DREW WITH A MAPPING PEN.

Y...YOU PULLED OUT THE *BACKGROUND CATALOG* BOOKS YOU FOUND IN THE REFERENCE MATERIAL BOXES AND USED THOSE TO DRAW THESE, RIGHT?
FOOM
YEAH, I PULLED THEM ALL OUT AND PLACED THEM ON THE SHELF NEAR THE DESK.
背景カタログ
(BOOKS: BACKGROUND CATALOG)
I NEVER KNEW THERE WAS SO MUCH REFERENCE MATERIAL FOR MANGA UNTIL I CAME HERE.
THESE DAYS, YOU CAN FIND LOTS OF IMAGES ON THE COMPUTER, BUT SINCE THESE COME WITH LINE DRAWINGS, YOU CAN EASILY REPLICATE THEM.
背景カタログ
13 学園生活編
SO WHAT DO YOU MEAN BY "EFFECTS"?
YOU DIDN'T SEE THEM INSIDE ALL THE DESK DRAWERS?
KLAT

WSH
THESE.
MY UNCLE WOULD TELL HIS ASSISTANTS WHICH EFFECTS TO DRAW USING THESE NUMBERS, BUT I'VE GOT TO BE ABLE TO DRAW THEM MYSELF FIRST.
I FOUND A BOOK CALLED *MANGA TECHNIQUES* THAT TEACHES YOU HOW TO DRAW THESE, BUT I HAVEN'T GIVEN IT A TRY YET.
MANGA TECHNIQUES
HOW TO DRAW MANGA
VOL. 1
ink
MONO
THERE'S NO WAY YOU CAN GET THAT FAR IN A DAY.
I'VE GOT TO PASTE THE SCREENTONES MYSELF TOO.
WOW... THERE'S SO MUCH YOU'VE GOT TO DO.

YEAH. I PANICKED A BIT AFTER REALIZING HOW MANY THINGS I HAVE TO MASTER BEFORE I CAN CREATE SOMETHING TO SUBMIT TO A PUBLISHER.
DRAWING STATIONARY PEOPLE IS EASY, BUT I HAVE TO COME UP WITH THEIR MOVES, EXPRESSION AND COMPOSITION INSIDE MY HEAD.
C SCREEN
IT'S NOTHING LIKE DRAWING A STILL LIFE PAINTING OR A LANDSCAPE PAINTING... I'VE GOT NO IDEA HOW LONG IT'S GOING TO TAKE...
NOW THAT I THINK OF IT, IT'S AMAZING HOW MY UNCLE MADE HIS DEBUT IN THREE YEARS CONSIDERING HOW HE STARTED OUT AS A COMPLETE AMATEUR.
NOT ONLY DID HE NOT KNOW ABOUT THE G-PEN, BUT HE DIDN'T EVEN KNOW ABOUT USING WHITEOUT. HE'D REDRAW THE ENTIRE PAGE IF HE MADE THE SMALLEST MISTAKE.
THAT'S STUPID BUT AMAZING...

GETTING OUR MANGA ANIMATED BY THE TIME WE'RE 18 YEARS OLD...
I CAN'T WASTE A SECOND OF MY TIME!
EVEN A SECOND...
EEE...
SAIKO...
HN?
I UNDERSTAND HOW YOU FEEL, BUT YOU SHOULD AT LEAST STUDY THE DAY BEFORE AN EXAM.
YEAH, I KNOW. I WAS GOING TO STUDY A BIT LAST NIGHT, BUT...
...IT WAS ALREADY MORNING BY THE TIME I NOTICED...
CHIRP
CHIRP

I'M ALREADY THINKING ABOUT JUST GOING TO YAKUSA NORTH FOR HIGH SCHOOL.
SHMP
NORTH HIGH?!
IT'S A HIGH SCHOOL FOR IDIOTS FROM YOUR POINT-OF-VIEW SINCE YOU GET THE HIGHEST GRADES IN SCHOOL, BUT THAT'S THE LOWEST LEVEL OF HIGH SCHOOL MY PARENTS WILL ALLOW ME TO ATTEND.
I'D RATHER ATTEND A LOW-LEVEL HIGH SCHOOL SO I DON'T HAVE TO STUDY MUCH. I'LL GET TO SPEND MY TIME DRAWING MANGA.
YAKUSA NORTH...
BUT IF THAT'S SAIKO'S DECISION, THERE'S NOTHING I CAN DO ABOUT IT... IT'S ALL FOR THE SAKE OF BECOMING A MANGA ARTIST...
BUT SAIKO, DON'T YOU NEED TO GO TO THE SAME HIGH SCHOOL AS AZUKI?
I DON'T KNOW WHICH HIGH SCHOOL SHE'S THINKING ABOUT, AND IT MAY TURN OUT TO BE A GIRL'S SCHOOL.
JUST ASK HER. HURRY UP AND GET HER EMAIL ADDRESS SO YOU CAN ASK.
NO, I'M GOING TO A DIFFERENT HIGH SCHOOL.
THAT WAY...
WRRL
WRRL

...IT'S MORE ROMANTIC.
WRRL
WRRL
THERE IT IS.
THE BLOOD OF A ROMANTICIST.
WRRL
WRRL
I GRADUATE MIDDLE SCHOOL, AND THE NEXT TIME I SEE AZUKI WILL BE...
Graduation Ceremony
...WHEN I'VE BECOME A MANGA ARTIST AND WHEN SHE'S BECOME A VOICE ACTRESS...
AND UNTIL THEN, YOU'RE GONNA ENCOURAGE EACH OTHER THROUGH TEXT MESSAGES AND EMAIL...
You can do it.
YEAH.
HEY... YOU DON'T HAVE TO IMITATE EVERYTHING YOUR UNCLE DID, DO YOU?
VSH
I'M NOT IMITATING HIM.
VSH
THIS IS WHAT I WANT TO DO.
VSH
I'M SURE THAT'S WHAT AZUKI WANTS TO DO TOO.
...
VSH

SAIKO, YOU HAVEN'T THOUGHT ABOUT HOW AZUKI MIGHT FIND HERSELF A BOYFRIEND IN HIGH SCHOOL, HAVE YOU?
VSH VSH VSH
WHY SHOULD I?
I TRUST HER.
I JUST DON'T UNDERSTAND HOW YOU CAN TRUST HER SO MUCH WHEN YOU HAVEN'T EVEN TALKED TO HER...
I USED TO JUST THINK, "I HOPE YOU TWO WILL MARRY EACH OTHER"...
...BUT FOR SOME REASON I NOW THINK, "YOU TWO REALLY ARE GOING TO MARRY EACH OTHER."
OF COURSE WE WILL.
SKREE
SO YOU'RE BOTH GOING TO REMAIN PURE AND CHASTE UNTIL THEN, HUH.
I DON'T GET HOW YOU CAN SAY EMBARRASSING THINGS LIKE THAT WITH A STRAIGHT FACE.
BUT THAT WOULD BE IDEAL, RIGHT? THAT'S WHAT YOU WANT, ISN'T IT, SAIKO?
WELL, YEAH, I GUESS THAT WOULD BE ABOUT RIGHT.
ABOUT RIGHT...?

BOTH AZUKI AND I WOULD BE 18 YEARS OLD...
EIGHTEEN IS ABOUT THE RIGHT AGE FOR THINGS LIKE THAT.
AH HA HA HA
HA HA HAA
DREAMS DON'T COME TRUE IF YOU JUST THINK ABOUT THEM.
I'VE GOT TO PRACTICE MY DRAWING.
VSH VSH VSH
...
SIGH... NORTH HIGH, HUH?
I'LL BE GOING THERE TOO THEN.
WHAAAT?!
YOU SHOULD BE GOING TO A HIGH-LEVEL SCHOOL, SHUJIN.
IT DOESN'T MAKE SENSE FOR YOU TO ATTEND NORTH HIGH.
NO.

IF WE'RE GOING TO BECOME A MANGA TEAM TOGETHER, IT'LL HAPPEN A LOT EASIER AND QUICKER IF WE ATTEND THE SAME HIGH SCHOOL.
I FEEL THE SAME WAY ABOUT NOT WANTING TO WASTE MY TIME, SAIKO.
PLUS...
...I WAS REALLY HAPPY WHEN YOU GAVE ME THE SPARE KEY TO THIS PLACE.
THAT'S THE LEAST I CAN DO TO REPAY YOU FOR THAT.
I WAS THINKING ABOUT ATTENDING TOKYO UNIVERSITY ONE DAY UNTIL I DECIDED TO TEAM UP WITH YOU...
SO HE REALLY WAS AIMING HIGH...
BUT IT'S UNCOOL TO BE A MANGA ARTIST WHO'S A TOKYO UNIVERSITY GRADUATE. YOU KNOW HOW PEOPLE CALL COMEDIANS WHO GRADUATE FROM TOKYO UNIVERSITY "I.Q. COMEDIANS" AND MAKE FUN OF THEM IF THEY'RE NOT FUNNY.
SO IT'S A LOT SAFER IF I GO TO A MEDIOCRE COLLEGE.
YOU JUST HAVE TO HIDE YOUR ACADEMIC BACK-GROUND, THAT'S ALL...
YOU'RE THE ONE WHO TOLD ME THAT YOU WERE GOING TO A GOOD COLLEGE AS INSURANCE IN CASE YOU COULDN'T BECOME A MANGA WRITER, REMEMBER?

SO NORTH HIGH IT IS. DON'T YOU FAIL NOW, SAIKO.
OF COURSE I WON'T. IT'S STUPID NORTH HIGH. STUPID NORTH...
HA HA HA HA
I SHOULDN'T BE THINKING ABOUT HOW I MIGHT FAIL, SHOULD I.
ANYWAY...
SINCE I'LL BE WRITING THE STORY, I WAS THINKING ABOUT READING ALL THE MANGA HERE, BUT...
WHAT DO YOU THINK? THERE ARE TENS OF THOUSANDS OF MANGA HERE...
HMM. I DON'T THINK YOU NEED TO READ ALL OF THEM, BUT YOU SHOULD AT LEAST READ THE ONES THAT ARE GOOD.
OH, YOU SHOULD START WITH *THE QUALIFICATIONS OF A MAN*. It should be around here somewhere.
WHAT'S THAT? IS IT INTER-ESTING?
(BOOKS BEING PULLED OUT: *THE QUALIFICATIONS OF A MAN*)
男の条件
男の条件
IT'S BASICALLY A "THIS IS WHAT A MANGA ARTIST SHOULD BE LIKE." IT'S WRITTEN BY IKKI KAJIWARA, THE GREATEST WRITER IN SHONEN MANGA HISTORY.
A REALLY OLD MANGA FROM THE '60S, I THINK. IT'S OUT OF PRINT NOW.
OOH! I'LL START WITH THAT THEN.

FROM *THE QUALIFICATIONS OF A MAN* (STORY BY: IKKI KAJIWARA / ART BY: NOBORU KAWASAKI)

THE THREE MAJOR QUALIFICATIONS FOR A MANGA ARTIST WHO ISN'T A GENIUS...
QUALIFICATION 1.
CONCEIT.
SERIOUSLY BELIEVE THAT YOU ARE BETTER THAN OTHERS.
YEAH, I'VE GOT THAT. BUT THEN AGAIN, I'M NOT BEING CONCEITED. I REALLY DO HAVE THE TALENT...
THAT'S WHAT YOU CALL BEING CONCEITED.
QUALIFICATION 2.
DO YOUR BEST.
OH, THAT'S A VERY DECENT THING FOR TARO KAWAGUCHI TO SAY.
AND LAST BUT NOT LEAST...
YEAH...?
LUCK.
WHAT?
SO IT ALL JUST BOILS DOWN TO LUCK?
OF COURSE. WE'RE NOT GENIUSES, AND THIS IS A GAMBLE.

SKRCH
SKRCH
EVERY DAY AFTER THAT, I PRACTICED DRAWING WHILE SHUJIN READ MANGA.
OHH.
THIS THE SOUL OF MY FATHER BRINGS TEARS TO MY EYES...
AND ON MONDAY, SHUJIN AND I WERE FACED WITH A BIT OF A SHOCK.
SAIKO!
HEY... C'MERE.
?
LOOK AT THIS.
SEMI-FINALIST!!
THE 76th
Tezuka Award Results
Prize: 1,000,000 yen Semi-Finalist
Large bander
Author: Eiji Nizuma (15) Aomori Prefecture
OH.
A SEMI-FINALIST FOR THE TEZUKA AWARD. THAT'S NOTHING SPECIAL, IS IT?
HIS AGE!
FIFTEEN YEARS OLD... HE'S IN THE SAME GRADE AS US OR MAYBE JUST A GRADE HIGHER!!

OHBA'S STORYBOARD

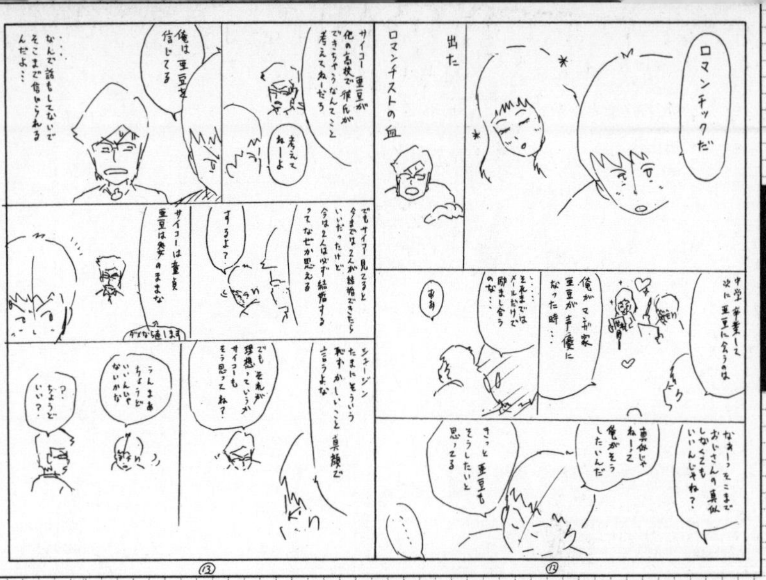

OBATA'S STORYBOARD

COMPLETE!

*CREATOR STORYBOARDS AND FINISHED PAGES IN JAPANESE

BAKUMAN。vol.1

"Until the Final Draft Is Complete"

Chapter 5, pp. 156-157

※JAPANESE MANGA AWARDS DON'T ALWAYS HAVE A FINALIST. IN THIS CASE, EIJI ACTUALLY RECEIVED THE TOP HONOR EVEN THOUGH HE DIDN'T WIN THE GRAND PRIZE.

WE'LL BE ABLE TO SURPASS THIS GUY QUICKLY.
IF YOU LOOK CARE-FULLY, THE JUDGES ONLY PRAISE HIS ARTWORK.
...
IT SOUNDS LIKE HE'S SAYING IT TO ME DIRECTLY 'CAUSE I WAS PLAYING VIDEO GAMES UNTIL A WEEK AGO.
YOU SURE DO SOUND CONFIDENT, SHUJIN.
IT'S "CONCEIT," NOT "CONFIDENCE."
REMEMBER, IT'S "CONFIDENCE," "DO YOUR BEST" AND "LUCK."
BUT "CONFIDENCE" SOUNDS BETTER. ANYWAY, IT MEANS THE SAME THING.
WEEKLY JUMP
THIS WEEK'S *KOCHI-KAME* IS REALLY FUNNY.

THERE ARE ACTUALLY QUITE A LOT OF GUYS AROUND OUR AGE WHO WANT TO BECOME MANGA ARTISTS.
GUYS IN CLASS 1...
YOU MEAN LIKE ISHIZAWA?
HE'D NEVER MAKE IT AS A MANGA ARTIST. I WAS IN THE SAME CLASS AS HIM FOR TWO YEARS...
HE JUST SHOWS OFF HOW HE CAN DRAW SO THAT PEOPLE WILL PAY ATTENTION TO HIM.
How cute!
Draw me next!
AND HE DOESN'T ACTUALLY DRAW MANGA. HE JUST DRAWS ILLUSTRATIONS OF WEIRD CUTESY-LOOKING GIRLS, SO I NEVER THOUGHT ABOUT TEAMING UP WITH HIM.
HE WAS LIKE THAT WHEN I WAS IN THE SAME CLASS AS HIM TOO.
HE CAN ONLY DRAW THE SAME THING OVER AND OVER AGAIN, YET HE CRITICIZES PROFES-SIONAL MANGA ARTISTS ALL THE TIME.
IT'S POINTLESS FOR US TO LOOK DOWN AND MAKE FUN OF HIM THOUGH.
RIGHT. FOR THE TIME BEING, OUR RIVAL IS EIJI.

I BET EIJI IS ALREADY TALKING WITH HIS SUPERVISING EDITOR ABOUT STARTING A SERIES AFTER HE GRADUATES HIGH SCHOOL OR SOMETHING LIKE THAT.
WHAT?! YOU THINK HE'S ALREADY GOT AN EDITOR?
I'M 100 PERCENT SURE HE'S GOT ONE. YOU GET ONE AUTOMATICALLY IF YOU RECEIVE AN AWARD. AND EVEN IF YOU DON'T GET AN AWARD, IF THERE'S AN EDITOR THAT LIKES YOUR WORK, HE'LL READILY BECOME YOUR SUPERVISOR.
MY UNCLE TOLD ME THAT WHEN I WAS IN 6TH GRADE. I'M SURE IT'S STILL THE SAME WAY.
RECEIVE AN AWARD
EDITOR
REJECTED
BUT I PERSONALLY LIKE YOUR WORK A LOT.
EDITOR
EDITOR, HUH. I'M STARTING TO FEEL A BIT ENVIOUS OF HIM...
WELL, MY UNCLE SAID THAT YOU JUST CAN'T BE HAPPY HAVING ONE SINCE THERE ARE ALWAYS GOING TO BE TOP EDITORS AND BOTTOM ONES.
WHAT DO YOU MEAN?
ROOKIES ARE ESPECIALLY INFLUENCED BY WHAT THEIR EDITOR TELLS THEM, SO IT'S BETTER TO BE ABLE TO DRAW WHAT YOU WANT RATHER THAN GET A BAD EDITOR.
MANGA ARTISTS CAN'T CHOOSE THEIR EDITORS THOUGH, SO WHETHER YOU GET A GOOD EDITOR OR NOT DEPENDS ON YOUR LUCK.
SO THAT'S WHERE LUCK COMES IN...
WHAT DO YOU MEAN BY TOP EDITORS AND BOTTOM ONES EXACTLY?

THINK OF THIS AS AN URBAN LEGEND. DON'T WRITE ABOUT IT ONLINE OR ANYTHING...
OOH, THIS IS GETTING EXCITING.
THERE'S THE TYPE OF EDITOR WHO YOU CAN'T GET IN TOUCH WITH DURING THE DAY, AND WHENEVER YOU GET IN TOUCH WITH HIM AT NIGHT, HE'S ALWAYS AT SOME HOSTESS BAR...
WHAT'D YOU SAY? I CAN'T HEAR YOU...
HA HA HA
SERIOUSLY?
I SAID TO THINK OF IT AS AN URBAN LEGEND, DIDN'T I?
THAT SUCKS...
AND HE'S ONE OF THE BETTER ONES 'CAUSE HE ACTUALLY CAME TO PICK THE FINAL DRAFT UP...
WHAT? THERE ARE ONES WHO ARE WORSE? WAIT, SAIKO, YOU SOUND LIKE YOUR UNCLE TOOK OVER YOUR BODY JUST NOW...
OH, SORRY. IT'S DEPRESSING TO LIST ALL THE BAD EXAMPLES, SO LET'S NOT TALK ABOUT THEM.
BUT I WANT TO HEAR MORE...
THEN I'LL TELL YOU ABOUT AN EDITOR THAT MOVED ME.
YEAH!

THERE WAS A ROOKIE WHO HAD DONE A ONE-SHOT FOR A DIFFERENT MAGAZINE BEFORE. THIS EDITOR TOLD HIM THAT HE HAD POTENTIAL AND TO COME BY WITH AS MANY FINAL DRAFTS AS HE COULD. AFTER AROUND THE TENTH TIME THE ROOKIE SUBMITTED A FINAL DRAFT, THE EDITOR READ THROUGH IT...
TAP TAP
...AND PLACED IT INTO A SHREDDER WITHOUT SAYING ANYTHING. HE SHREDDED THAT FINAL DRAFT RIGHT IN FRONT OF THE ROOKIE.
SHWRR
THAT'S AWFUL!
WHAAT?!
IT'S GREAT HOW STRICT THE EDITOR WAS WITH THE ROOKIE.
WHAT'S SO MOVING ABOUT THAT?
YOU CAN GET SUED FOR DOING SOMETHING LIKE THAT NOWADAYS. IT'S WAY WORSE THAN LOSING A FINAL DRAFT.
BEFORE THAT, THE EDITOR HAD BEEN SAYING "NO GOOD" AFTER ONLY READING THE FIRST FEW PAGES OF THE DRAFTS, SO THE ROOKIE WAS REALLY HAPPY WHEN THE EDITOR FINALLY READ ALL THE PAGES. BUT WHEN THE EDITOR SHREDDED THOSE PAGES IN FRONT OF HIM, THE ROOKIE GOT FRUS-TRATED AND WORKED EVEN HARDER. HE EVENTUALLY BECAME ONE OF THE TOP MANGA ARTISTS.
AH, IT'S FINALLY STARTING TO SOUND LIKE A GOOD STORY. THE ROOKIE DIDN'T GIVE UP, AND HE WORKED HARDER TO GET BACK AT THE EDITOR.
SKRCH
SKRCH

LATER ON, WHILE THE TWO OF THEM WERE HAVING A MEETING ABOUT A MANGA THAT WAS BEING SERIALIZED, THE EDITOR SAID, "THAT WORK I SHREDDED WAS GOOD TOO, BUT I KNEW YOU'D BECOME EVEN BETTER IF I DIDN'T COMMEND YOUR WORK BACK THEN. THAT'S WHY I ACTED ON IMPULSE." THEN HE APOLOGIZED.
I'm sorry about that.
Thank you so much.
AND THE MANGA ARTIST THANKED HIM FOR DOING IT.
TH... THAT SOUNDS TOTALLY MADE-UP! IT'S LIKE A SCENE OUT OF SOME MANGA.
I'M SURE MY UNCLE HEARD IT FROM SOMEBODY. MAYBE THE STORY'S MADE-UP...
...BUT THAT EDITOR ENDED UP BECOMING THE EDITOR IN CHIEF.
WHAT I WANT TO SAY IS THAT MOST OF THE EDITORS HAVE A VERY STRONG PASSION FOR MANGA.
RIGHT... I WANT THEM TO BE THAT WAY. BUT I DON'T WANT THEM TO SHRED MY WORK EITHER.
HAVE YOU EVER MET AN EDITOR BEFORE, SAIKO?
NOPE. I WASN'T ALLOWED INSIDE THE OFFICE WHEN THE EDITOR WAS THERE.
WHY DON'T WE GO MEET ONE?
KOFF

IF YOU CALL THEM UP AND SAY, "THERE'S A PIECE OF WORK I'D LIKE TO SUBMIT," THEY SEE YOU, RIGHT?
YEAH, THEY DO, BUT WE DON'T HAVE ANYTHING TO SUBMIT YET.
...
SAIKO... IF WE'RE GOING TO PUBLISH A SERIES, IT SHOULD BE IN *JUMP*, RIGHT?
YEAH. WE WANT TO GET OUR MANGA ANIMATED, SO *JUMP* WOULD BE THE BEST PLACE TO START.
I ALSO THINK WE SHOULD HAVE A SERIES IN *JUMP* IF WE'RE AIMING TO BECOME THE BEST IN JAPAN.
WHICH MEANS...
...AS LONG AS IT'S NOT THE *JUMP* EDITORIAL OFFICE AT SHUEISHA, WE CAN JUST SLAP TOGETHER ANY KIND OF WORK, RIGHT?
WE JUST SUBMIT IT SOMEWHERE AND SEE WHAT THE EDITOR THERE THINKS OF THAT PIECE.
...

I COME UP WITH SOME RANDOM STORY, AND YOU DRAW SOME RANDOM ILLUSTRATIONS.
WE'LL GET TO TOUR AN EDITORIAL OFFICE. LIKE RECONNAISSANCE.
...
...
OKAY, FORGET ABOUT IT.
I JUST WANNA SEE WHAT IT'S LIKE, BUT I'M SURE YOU DON'T WANT TO DRAW SOME RANDOM STUFF...
NO.
FUP...
YOU REALLY ARE SMART, SHUJIN. LET'S PUT TOGETHER A FINAL DRAFT AND TAKE IT DOWN TO *SHONEN THREE*!
Ha ha!
SSUUU
IN THAT CASE, LET'S HEAD TO THE STUDIO.
I'VE ALREADY GOT A STORY IN MY HEAD.
DASH
OH, IS IT THIS LATE ALREADY? I'LL HAVE TO CALL MY PARENTS AND TELL THEM I'LL BE EATING OUT.
I'VE BEEN DOING THAT LATELY TOO.
PAYING 280 YEN* TO RIDE THE TRAIN IS STARTING TO GET TO ME... MAYBE I'LL GET A TRAIN PASS OR RIDE MY BICYCLE...
HEY, THREE BEAUTIFUL WOMEN UP AHEAD.
HUH?

*ABOUT $3

AZUKI ...
I HEARD SHE HAS A YOUNGER SISTER IN 5TH GRADE. SHE'S CUTE TOO.
SHOOT, WHAT DO I DO?
WHAT'S WRONG? NOW'S YOUR CHANCE TO GET HER EMAIL ADDRESS.
DON'T BE ABSURD. SHE'S WITH THAT INTIMIDATING MOTHER OF HERS.
WHAT, LIKE YOU CAN ASK HER WHEN YOU'RE ALONE WITH HER?
SHUT UP.

LET'S JUST PRETEND NOT TO NOTICE THEM AND WALK PAST.
I DON'T THINK THAT'S REALLY POSSIBLE.
JUST DO IT.
OH, IT LOOKS LIKE AZUKI NOTICED YOU TOO.
SHE'S OBVIOUSLY BLUSHING. NOW SHE'S TRYING TO HIDE BEHIND HER MOTHER.
SHU...
YOU DON'T HAVE TO GIVE ME THE PLAY-BY-PLAY, SHUJIN...

WHAT A COINCIDENCE, MIHO. ISN'T THAT YOUR CLASSMATE?
!
!
PFFT...
OOH, YOUR FACE IS ALL RED, SIS.
SHUT UP, MINA. I DON'T WANT THEM TO SEE ME WITH MOM, THAT'S ALL.
YOU TWO ARE SO SHY...
I'M AMAZED AT HOW YOU'RE ABLE TO IGNORE EACH OTHER IN CLASS.
SHUT UP.

READ THIS WAY
PHEW... I KNEW HER MOM WAS GOING TO SAY SOMETHING UNNECESSARY.
"WHAT A COINCIDENCE," MY FOOT...
HA HA
YEAH, I COULD BARELY KEEP MYSELF FROM LAUGHING.
...
I GATHERED ALL THE COURAGE I HAD INSIDE ME AND LOOKED BACK...
AND BY SOME STRANGE CHANCE, AZUKI LOOKED BACK TOO.
TIME STOPPED, AND EVERYTHING AROUND ME TURNED TRANSPARENT.

THIS 0.1 SECOND FELT LIKE TEN SECONDS, AND I QUICKLY LOOKED FORWARD.
A COUPLE OF SECONDS LATER, I TURNED AROUND AGAIN.
I COULD SEE AZUKI LOOKING BACK AGAIN TOO.
SHE AND I HAD THE EXACT SAME FREQUENCY.

FREQUENCY?
IT COULD JUST BE THAT AZUKI TURNED AROUND TEN TIMES, AND YOU JUST HAPPENED TO SEE HER TURN AROUND TWO OF THOSE TIMES.
SCRTCH SCRTCH
NO WAY.
WELL, I DON'T UNDERSTAND THIS "FREQUENCY" FEELING OF YOURS... SO THE ONLY THING I CAN SAY IS THAT I'M JEALOUS.
WRRL WRRL
UH-HUH.
THE FIRST TIME I MET AZUKI WAS IN 6TH GRADE.
I WAS IN MEIYO ELEMENTARY SCHOOL, BUT SHE WAS IN MEIYO 2 ELEMENTARY.
DURING THE INTERSCHOLASTIC SWIMMING TOURNAMENT, AZUKI AND I JUST KEPT STARING AT EACH OTHER FROM DIFFERENT SIDES.
I GUESS WE WEREN'T EMBARRASSED TO DO THAT BACK THEN.

ENTRANCE CEREMONY
OUR EYES MET AGAIN AT THE SCHOOL GATE DURING THE DAY OF OUR ENTRANCE CEREMONY.
WE WERE STANDING CLOSE TO EACH OTHER THEN, SO WE QUICKLY TURNED OUR FACES AWAY.
SO YOU GUYS WERE IN LOVE WITH EACH OTHER SINCE ELEMENTARY SCHOOL?
I'M ONLY RECALLING THESE INCIDENTS NOW.
SKRCH
SKRCH
GOT IT. WELL, EVEN IF YOU GUYS HAVE SOME SORT OF FREQUENCY GOING ON, YOU'RE NOT GOING TO BE ABLE TO COMMUNICATE IF YOU DON'T EXCHANGE EMAIL ADDRESSES.
UNLESS YOU GUYS CAN DO TELEPATHY BY SYNCHRONIZING YOUR FREQUENCIES OR SOMETHING.
I'LL BE FINE AS LONG AS I CAN EXCHANGE ADDRESSES BY THE TIME WE GRADUATE. I WANT TO CONCENTRATE ON MANGA FOR NOW.
OKAY. HERE'RE THE FIRST FIVE PAGES.
THAT WAS FAST.
SHU
Double Earth The Two Earths
TITLE, "DOUBLE EARTH, THE TWO EARTHS"...
THE "DOUBLE EARTH" PART IS A JOKE. TAKE THAT OFF.
Double Earth
The Two Earths

Real Earth
The Earth we live in is nothing but a clone of the real Earth.
Our Earth
And we humans are nothing but clones of the humans living on the real Earth.
2
We are nothing but guinea pigs created by the real humans for their experiments.
By leaving us clones in the exact same environment as them, they are using us to make their world better.
There is no such thing as war or global warming in the real Earth because we have provided them with those results.
3
SHUJIN...
HM? SORRY, I DIDN'T HAVE MUCH TIME, SO I DREW VERY LARGE PANELS. I'LL BE INCLUDING LOADS OF RANDOM TWO-PAGE SPREADS TOO.
SKRCH
SKRCH
DID YOU RIP THIS STORY OFF OF SOMETHING?
IT'S NOT A RIP-OFF OF ANYTHING SPECIFIC, BUT IT'S ONE OF THOSE STORIES THAT ANYBODY WOULD COME UP WITH. SORRY IF THERE ARE PARTS THAT SEEM SIMILAR TO SOMETHING YOU KNOW... TO TELL YOU THE TRUTH, THIS IS THE BEST I CAN DO FOR NOW...

THIS ISN'T SOMETHING JUST ANYBODY WOULD THINK OF. I'D NEVER COME UP WITH SOMETHING LIKE THIS FOR SURE. THERE ARE SERIES IN MAGAZINES THAT HAVE IDEAS STOLEN FROM OTHER MANGA AS WELL AS VIDEO GAMES, YOU KNOW.
I REALLY LIKE THIS STORY YOU'VE WRITTEN.
REALLY?
REALLY.
BUT ALL THAT'S LEFT OF THE STORY IS HOW THE HUMANS FROM THE CLONE EARTH ARE FIGHTING THE HUMANS FROM THE REAL EARTH...
Real Earth
IT'S INTERESTING BECAUSE YOU CAN SEE THAT COMING. WE CAN CREATE A FULL-FLEDGED WAR BETWEEN THE HUMANS.
HEY... WHY DON'T WE DO THIS PROPERLY AND TAKE IT DOWN TO THE *JUMP* EDITORIAL OFFICE? I PROMISE YOU THAT I'LL DO MY BEST WITH THE ARTWORK.
OH...
OR DO YOU HAVE SOMETHING BETTER THAN THIS IN MIND?
MM... WELL, I DID THINK OF A SPORTS MANGA TOO. **"SUNGLASS PITCHER"** ...
A FAST-PITCH ELEMENTARY SCHOOL STUDENT WHO HAS DREAMS OF BECOMING A PROFESSIONAL BASEBALL PLAYER LOSES HIS EYESIGHT ONE DAY AFTER GETTING A LINE-DRIVE COME-BACKER TO THE FACE.
TEN YEARS LATER, A MYSTERIOUS PITCHER WEARING SUNGLASSES APPEARS IN THE PROFESSIONAL BASEBALL WORLD AND PITCHES A PERFECT GAME WITH HIS PERFECTLY-CONTROLLED 112 MPH FASTBALL.

THE BOY HAD NOT GIVEN UP HIS DREAM AND HAD BEEN SECRETLY TRAINING WITH HIS FATHER FOR THE LAST TEN YEARS.
Next, 38!
Yes!
SHA
THE BASEBALL ASSOCIATION FINDS OUT THAT HE'S BLIND AND TRIES TO THROW HIM OUT, BUT HE CONTINUES TO FIGHT HIS RIVALS WHO ALL WANT TO DEFEAT HIM.
...
YOU REALLY ARE TALENTED, SHUJIN.
PEOPLE NORMALLY DON'T THINK ABOUT SO MANY DETAILS WHEN THEY CREATE A STORY! THEY START TO THINK IT SOUNDS TOO STUPID AND END UP STOPPING! BUT UNFOLDING THAT SEEMINGLY STUPID STORY WILL–
S-SERIOUSLY? DO YOU REALLY THINK I'VE GOT TALENT?!
I... I'M SO GLAD TO HEAR THAT... TO TELL YOU THE TRUTH, I'VE BEEN FORCING MYSELF TO COME UP WITH A STORY EVERY DAY NOW ...
BUT I TEND TO BE OVER-CONFIDENT ABOUT MYSELF, SO I WAS REALLY WORRIED ABOUT WHAT YOU'D THINK...
IT'S REALLY REASSURING TO HEAR THAT YOU LIKE IT, SAIKO. I'M REALLY, REALLY GLAD...
And you said you like sports manga!
SHUJIN...
I CONVINCED SHUJIN TO CREATE A PROPER FINAL DRAFT BASED ON "THE TWO EARTHS" BY THE END OF SUMMER BREAK SO THAT WE COULD TAKE IT DOWN TO THE JUMP EDITORIAL OFFICE.
SO THE IDEAL LENGTH WOULD BE 31 TO 45 PAGES?
YEAH, THAT SOUNDS ABOUT RIGHT!

OHBA'S STORYBOARD

OBATA'S STORYBOARD

COMPLETE!

*CREATOR STORYBOARDS AND FINISHED PAGES IN JAPANESE

BAKUMAN。 vol. 1

"Until the Final Draft Is Complete"

Chapter 6, pp. 178-179

AFTER WE DECIDED TO TAKE OUR FINAL DRAFT TO JUMP BY THE END OF SUMMER BREAK...
I'M GOING TO HAVE TO FINISH THAT STORYBOARD. BUT NO MATTER HOW MANY TIMES I REWRITE IT, I JUST DON'T LIKE HOW THE LAST HALF TURNS OUT.
SKR
SKR
MI
MI
CHAPTER 7
SMILE AND BASHFUL
MY DRAWINGS AREN'T GOOD ENOUGH YET FOR THE FINAL DRAFT...
SO AT WORST, I'LL BE FINE AS LONG AS YOU CAN FINISH THE LAST HALF WHILE I'M WORKING ON THE FIRST HALF.
...OUR TIME AT SCHOOL WAS THE ONLY TIME WE COULD RELAX AND TAKE IT EASY.

FOUND YOU.
ISN'T THAT MIYOSHI?
YUP, MIYOSHI. CLASS 1, NUMBER 31, KAYA MIYOSHI. BEST FRIEND OF MIHO AZUKI, CLASS 2, NUMBER 3.
TAKAGI, COME OVER HERE...
SHE'S CALLING FOR YOU.
I DON'T WANNA GO.
TMP TMP
I NEED TO TALK TO YOU.
WHAT?
IT'S OKAY, STAY.

MIHO GOT MAD AT ME THE OTHER DAY. SHE WAS LIKE, "HOW COME TAKAGI KNOWS ABOUT MY DREAM? YOU TOLD HIM, DIDN'T YOU?"
WHAT'S WRONG WITH THAT? I JUST WANTED TO ASK HER IN PERSON.
OH, BUT I DID TELL THIS GUY ABOUT IT. HE'S MY FRIEND, MASHIRO.
...
...
I TOLD YOU NOT TO TELL *ANYBODY* BECAUSE SHE'S REALLY BASHFUL.
OKAY, I WON'T TELL ANYBODY ELSE.
BUT YOU SHOULD TELL HER, "ARE YOU REALLY GOING TO BE ABLE TO BECOME A VOICE ACTRESS IF YOU'RE THAT BASHFUL?"
I'M NOT GONNA SAY THAT.
IN ANY CASE, I WON'T TELL ANYBODY ELSE, SO DON'T WORRY ABOUT IT.
SO DID MIHO DUMP YOU?
HUH? WHAT KIND OF JOKE IS THAT?
WELL, YOU TALKED TO HER, RIGHT?
I JUST WANTED TO CHECK WITH HER ABOUT THAT DREAM OF HERS. AND ANYWAY, SHE ALREADY HAS A GUY SHE LIKES.
NO WAY.
WHO?!
SHE DOESN'T KNOW...

I DON'T KNOW. BUT SHE'S A 3RD-YEAR, SO I'M SURE SHE HAS SOMEBODY IN MIND.
HMM... WELL, I GUESS A 3RD-YEAR GIRL WOULD HAVE SOMEBODY...
...BUT MIHO NEVER TALKS ABOUT THINGS LIKE THAT...
HEY, WHY DID YOU ASK ME ABOUT MIHO IN THE FIRST PLACE THEN?
HUH? WELL, THAT'S...
...BECAUSE I WANTED TO TALK TO YOU, MIYOSHI.
?
You've done it now, Shujin...
L... LET ME THINK IT OVER.
HUH?
HEY, MIYO...
TUG

READ THIS WAY

MIHO...
TAKAGI IN YOUR CLASS JUST TOLD ME HE HAS A CRUSH ON ME.
YOU'RE KIDDING.
SO TAKAGI AND KAYA TALKED TO EACH OTHER AGAIN...
I'M PRETTY SURE HE WON'T TELL HER ABOUT MASHIRO AND ME, BUT...

WHAT DO YOU THINK?
HUH? ABOUT WHAT?
TAKAGI!
WELL, HE'S SMART, HE'S GOOD AT SPORTS, HE'S TALL...
TH... THAT'S RIGHT... I'M NOT THE TYPE OF PERSON WHO'D LOOK GOOD TOGETHER WITH HIM.
THAT'S NOT TRUE.
EVERYBODY IN MY CLASS WAS SAYING TAKAGI'S GOING OUT WITH IWASE...
I DON'T THINK SHE'S VERY POPULAR WITH BOYS.
WHY NOT? SHE'S REALLY SMART AND PRETTY.
SHE PROBABLY COMES OFF AS A LITTLE SNOBBY TO THE BOYS...
AND I DON'T THINK BOYS CARE ABOUT WHETHER A GIRL LOOKS GOOD WITH THEM OR NOT. TAKAGI MUST THINK YOU'RE CUTE, KAYA.
I'M CUTE?
UH-HUH.

SO WHO'S THIS PERSON YOU HAVE A CRUSH ON, MIHO?
HUH?
I DON'T HAVE A CRUSH ON ANYONE.
I KNEW YOU'D SAY THAT. TAKAGI AND MASHIRO WERE SAYING THAT YOU DO THOUGH, AND I CAN SEE IT ON YOUR FACE TOO.
GEEZ... WHAT DID TAKAGI TELL HER? FROM THE WAY SHE'S TALKING, I DON'T THINK SHE KNOWS THAT IT'S MASHIRO...
SO WHO IS IT? WHO IS IT?
AH HA HA HA~!
THERE'S...
...NO ONE, I SAID.
TICKLE
TICKLE
NO ONE, HUH...
YOU KNOW...
YOU SAID IWASE'S SNOBBY, BUT I BET THE BOYS THINK YOU'RE SNOBBY TOO.
WHAT...?
I'VE KNOWN YOU FOR ABOUT FIVE YEARS NOW, BUT I'VE NEVER SEEN YOU TALKING TO A BOY. YOU'RE SUPER CUTE, BUT YOU WON'T TALK TO BOYS... DON'T YOU THINK THAT'S A BIT SNOBBY?
...

KAYA.
YES?
WRRL
I'M NOT SNOBBY, I'M JUST TOO EMBARRASSED TO TALK TO BOYS.
TO TELL YOU THE TRUTH, I LIKE BOYS MORE THAN YOU DO.
YEAH?
MAYBE IT'S BECAUSE I DON'T HAVE ANY MALE SIBLINGS, BUT I JUST START TURNING RED WHEN I TRY TO TALK TO BOYS. THAT'S WHY I CAN'T TALK TO THEM, UNDERSTAND?
...
IT'S FUNNY HOW YOU SOUND LIKE A TEACHER SOMETIMES, MIHO.
I KNOW YOU'RE BEING SERIOUS WHEN YOU TALK LIKE THAT, SO I KNOW YOU'RE NOT LYING.
DONG
DONG
OH, LUNCH BREAK IS OVER.
TAKAGI AND MASHIRO ARE BACK?!
SHA
DONG
DONG

IF YOU'RE GOING TO TELL TAKAGI YOU WANT TO GO OUT WITH HIM, YOU'LL HAVE TO SAY IT BY YOURSELF. I CAN'T DO IT WITH YOU.
WHAT?
THEN I'LL IGNORE HIM AND GO BACK TO MY CLASSROOM.
SEE YOU.
GLANCE
MAYBE OUR FREQUENCY WAS THE SAME?
SHE JUST TURNED AROUND.
WHAT AM I SUPPOSED TO DO IF SHE SAYS, "SURE, I'LL GO OUT WITH YOU"?
HAHA. "I WANT TO TALK TO YOU, BUT I CAN'T GO OUT WITH YOU..." THAT'S A LITTLE TOUGH, ISN'T IT.
IT'S NOT FUNNY, SAIKO...
THIS WAS PRETTY MUCH THE ONLY CHANGE THAT HAPPENED DURING MY FIRST SEMESTER.

READ THIS WAY
OH, ONE OTHER THING CHANGED...
SO IF YOU JUST REMEMBER THESE TWO FORMULAS, THEN YOU'LL BE ABLE TO SOLVE PRETTY MUCH EVERYTHING ON THESE PAGES.
I DON'T UNDERSTAND THIS AT ALL.
SHUJIN TAUGHT ME HOW TO GET GOOD GRADES BEFORE THE FINAL EXAM, SO MY GRADE RANKING FROM THE MIDTERM EXAMS OF 19TH ROSE TO 6TH.
Moritaka Mashiro
SHUJIN AND MIYOSHI SEEMED TO BE ATTRACTED TO EACH OTHER, BUT THEY DIDN'T START GOING OUT...
...AND I STARTED SUMMER BREAK WITHOUT EXCHANGING EMAIL ADDRESSES WITH AZUKI.
Summer Break

JIII
JIII
JIII
JIII
ONCE SUMMER BREAK STARTED, SHUJIN AND I CONVINCED OUR PARENTS TO LET US SLEEP OVER AT THE STUDIO.
I ONLY SLEPT FOUR HOURS A DAY LIKE A PROFES-SIONAL MANGA ARTIST.
SHUJIN FINISHED THE STORYBOARD AT THE BEGINNING OF AUGUST, SO HE GOT PLENTY OF SLEEP. IT WAS NOW UP TO ME TO DRAW THE FINAL DRAFT.
...
HE'S WORKING TOO HARD... HE'S GOING TO COLLAPSE AT THIS RATE.
IF WE CALL AZUKI, MAYBE SHE'LL COME DOWN HERE AND DO THE LAUNDRY, CLEAN AND COOK FOR US...
SHE COULD WEAR A MAID OUTFIT AND BE OUR RESIDENTIAL MAID. WHAT DO YOU THINK?
Your meal is ready, Master.
Oh...
Thank you...

I... I'M JUST JOKING!
HISS
SORRY! SHE ISN'T THAT KIND OF PERSON, I KNOW.
IT'S NO USE. HE WON'T EVEN LAUGH AT MY JOKES.
GAH
DID YOU FINISH MY HOMEWORK?
STAGGER
YEAH. YOU JUST NEED TO COPY IT. I EVEN MADE MISTAKES ON PURPOSE IN PLACES WHERE YOU'D PROBABLY MAKE MISTAKES.
THANKS FOR ALL YOUR HELP.
SKRITCH
FOOO
HEY, WE HAVE THE AC ON 24 HOURS A DAY. WHO'S PAYING THE UTILITY BILLS FOR THIS PLACE?
MY PARENTS OR MY GRANDPA.
SKRITCH
SKRATCH
WE HAVE TO PAY THEM BACK ONCE WE MAKE SOME MONEY... WELL, EVEN IF WE DON'T MAKE MONEY, WE SHOULD...
WE'RE GONNA MAKE MONEY, AND WE'RE GONNA PAY THEM BACK 100 TIMES WHAT THEY PAID FOR US.
R... RIGHT.
VWSH
SAIKO BECAME VERY SERIOUS AFTER READING THAT EDITION OF JUMP...
2008

BANG
EIJI NIZUMA'S TEZUKA AWARD-WINNING PIECE LARGE BANDER WAS PUBLISHED IN THAT ISSUE, AND IT WAS FAR BETTER THAN WHAT WE HAD EXPECTED.
IT'S TOO LATE!
LARGE VIRUS ONE HUNDRED THOUSAND TIMES
DESTRUCTION
KRAK
DUM DUM
LIVE...!!!!!!!
DESTRUCTION TRIGGER!!!
EVEN THE EVER CONFIDENT SHUJIN ADMITTED THAT EIJI WAS FAR BETTER THAN US AT THIS POINT.
I JUST COULDN'T ADMIT DEFEAT THOUGH. I FOUND OUT THAT I HAPPEN TO BE A VERY SORE LOSER WHEN IT COMES TO DRAWING.
URR
I KEPT THAT MOTIVATION UP AND STARTED ON THE FINISHING TOUCHES AROUND THE END OF AUGUST.
SHOULDN'T YOU SLEEP A BIT? WE STILL HAVE FOUR MORE DAYS OF SUMMER BREAK, YOU KNOW.
SHP SHP
NO, I'M GOING TO FINISH THIS.
HYUU
YES, I'M FINISHED WITH THE WHITEOUT! ALL I'VE GOT LEFT ARE THE SCREENTONES.
WSH
WHEW...
...
SHUP SHUP

SAIKO, YOU MIND IF I HELP?
I THOUGHT WE AGREED THAT I WOULDN'T MEDDLE WITH YOUR WRITING AND THAT YOU WOULDN'T MEDDLE WITH MY DRAWING.
OH, I JUST WANT TO WORK ON THE FINAL DRAFT SO THAT I CAN EXPERIENCE COMPLETING IT TOGETHER WITH YOU...
IS THAT OKAY?
SH
FINE. THEN I WANT YOU TO PASTE THIS ON TO EVERY ONE OF THE EARTH ARMY'S TROUSERS.
GOT IT, THANKS.
KRSH KRSH KRSH KRSH KRSH KRSH
THIS IS IT.
WE'RE GOING TO GO NON-STOP TO THE END NOW!
WE WORKED OVERNIGHT TO FINISH OUR WORK. ON AUGUST 28, 2008, THE TWO EARTHS WAS FINALLY COMPLETED.
W... WE DID IT...
HUFF
HUFF
PHEW...

IT MAY NOT BE AS GOOD AS EIJI'S, BUT IT'S A GREAT PIECE TO TAKE DOWN TO THE EDITORIAL OFFICE FOR THEM TO SEE WHAT WE'VE GOT.
The Two Earths
WE REALLY CAN DO IT IF WE GIVE IT EVERYTHING WE'VE GOT.
The Two Earths
I LIKE THE ARTWORK, BUT I'M NOT SURE ABOUT MY STORY.
I LIKE THE STORY, BUT I'M NOT SURE ABOUT MY ARTWORK.

SAIKO...
FWUP
FWUP
WH... WHAT? ISN'T THAT A LITTLE EMBARRASSING?
GRP
THANKS FOR EVERYTHING, SAIKO.
SHUJIN WAS CRYING A BIT, BUT I COULDN'T LAUGH AT THOSE TEARS.

O-OKAY, LET'S CALL SHUEISHA AND TELL THEM ABOUT THIS.
YOU CALL, SHUJIN.
CHAK
I HAD A FEELING YOU'D SAY THAT...
HAHR
YOU'RE GOOD AT TALKING TO ADULTS. YOU WERE GOOD WITH AZUKI'S MOM, REMEMBER?
I'M NOT THAT GOOD...
...
IF I CALL THEM FROM THIS PHONE, WON'T THEY BE LIKE, "A PHONE CALL FROM TARO KAWAGUCHI'S OFFICE! HE'S COME BACK FROM THE DEAD!"?
OF COURSE NOT. NOBODY PROBABLY REMEMBERS THIS NUMBER ANYWAY. IF YOU DON'T WANT TO USE THAT PHONE, THEN USE YOUR CELLPHONE.
HURRY UP.
FWMP
WHAT SHOULD I SAY?
NNGH...
SOMETHING LIKE, "I HAVE A PIECE I'D LIKE TO SUBMIT FOR YOUR CONSIDERATION."
YEAH, OKAY.
JII
JII
WE'RE TO GO DOWN TO THE FRONT DESK TOMORROW AT THREE O'CLOCK AND SAY THAT WE HAVE AN APPOINTMENT WITH MR. HATTORI OF *WEEKLY SHONEN JUMP*.
KLAK
TOMORROW? THAT SOON? WELL, IT'S BETTER TO GO BEFORE THE SECOND SEMESTER STARTS...
SHUP

(SIGN: SHUEISHA)

OHBA'S STORYBOARD

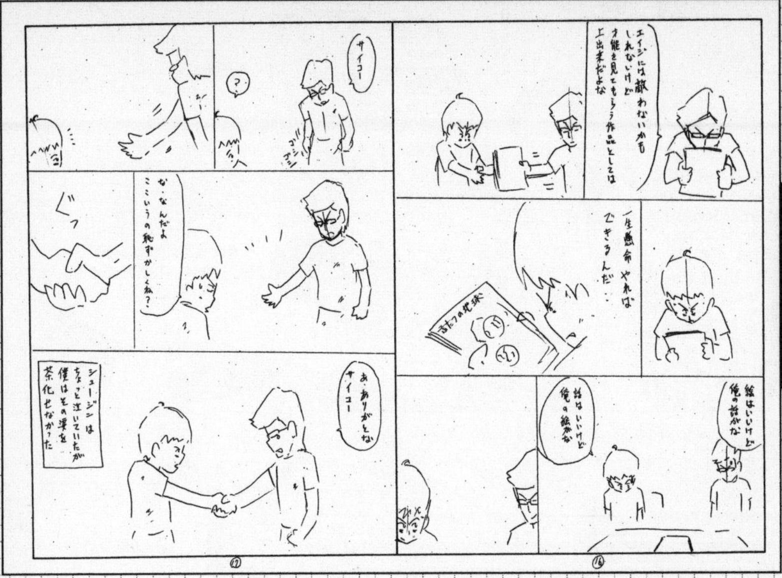

OBATA'S STORYBOARD

COMPLETE!

*CREATOR STORYBOARDS AND FINISHED PAGES IN JAPANESE

BAKUMAN。 vol. 1

"Until the Final Draft Is Complete"

Chapter 7, pp. 200-201

BAKUMAN。

In the NEXT VOLUME

What sort of reception will Moritaka and Akito's manga get from the editor at publishing company Shueisha?

Available Now!

This is the LAST PAGE.

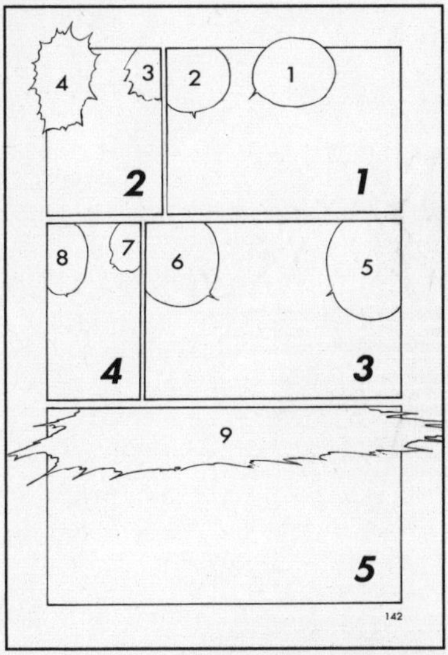

← Follow the action this way.

***BAKUMAN*。has been printed in the original Japanese format in order to preserve the orientation of the original artwork.**

Please turn it around and begin reading from right to left. Unlike English, Japanese is read right to left, so Japanese comics are read in reverse order from the way English comics are typically read. Have fun with it!